Mitsui Madhouse

Mitsui Madhouse

Memoir of a U.S. Army Air Corps POW in World War II

by HERBERT ZINCKE
with SCOTT A. MILLS

McFarland & Company, Inc., Publishers
Jefferson, North Carolina, and London

Frontispiece: Technical Sergeant Herbert Zincke, 1946.

Library of Congress Cataloguing-in-Publication Data

Zincke, Herbert 1919–
    Mitsui madhouse : memoir of a U.S. Army air corps POW in
World War II / by Herbert Zincke with Scott A. Mills.
      p.   cm.
    Includes bibliographical references and index.

    ISBN 0-7864-1428-6 (softcover: 50# alkaline paper)

    1. Zincke, Herbert, 1919–   2. World War, 1939–1945—Personal
narratives, American.   3. World War, 1939–1945—Prisoners and
prisons, Japanese.   4. Bomber pilots—United States—Biography.
5. Prisoners of war—Japan—Biography.   6. World War, 1939–
1945—Philippines.   I. Mills, Scott A., 1924–   II. Title.
D811.Z56   2003
940.54'7252'092—dc21   2002014548

British Library cataloguing data are available

On the cover: Sgt. Herbert Zincke, POW at Camp No. 2, Kawasaki,
July 10, 1943, superimposed upon B-29 Superfortresses flying over
Mt. Fujiyama (National Archives, 342-FH-3B25882-63370)

Manufactured in the United States of America

McFarland & Company, Inc., Publishers
  Box 611, Jefferson, North Carolina 28640
   www.mcfarlandpub.com

To my stepmother,
whose moral and spiritual guidance made possible my survival,
and to the soldiers, sailors, and marines
who gave their lives in defense of the Philippines.

Table of Contents

Preface

I spent almost three years at the Kawasaki slave labor camp on Tokyo Bay. The barracks building belonged to the Mitsui Corporation. We had been there only a few weeks when we named it the "Mitsui Madhouse"—most appropriate because of the crazy and brutal treatment being meted out by the soldiers and guards of the Japanese Army. Yet there are many true reports of worse treatment at the other 126 slave labor camps in Japan.

But the kind of brutality that occurred at our camp, and losses of life from malnutrition and medical neglect, probably happened at all of the camps. At Kawasaki we kept up our morale by sticking together in many different situations. For instance, a few men could always be counted upon to make a wisecrack when a fellow prisoner seemed about to fight back when pounded by Japanese blows. Such spontaneous efforts to protect each other still brighten my memories.

However, back home after the war I was so angry about what had happened that I didn't want to talk about the Mitsui Madhouse—even to my wonderful mother and aunt. When they gently enquired, I just clammed up, upset by the idea of recalling the camp. In a few years, though, I began to believe I had a story to tell and started to write something down. My story was based on the secret diary that I had been able to keep out of Japanese hands. But the diary brought back experiences that angered me all over again. I threw everything I had written into the fireplace; but before I could light a fire, my first wife noticed what I was doing and saved my work. Later, when my mood mellowed, I produced a complete account.

In recent years, Victor Mapes, a friend from our wartime 14th Air

Scott A. Mills (left) and Herbert
Zincke in 2001.

Corps Squadron, published the story of
his long imprisonment in the Philippines. His book made me think seriously about publishing my own account
of the three years I spent as a prisoner
in Japan. I was glad to have Scott A.
Mills, a Navy veteran of the Pacific war,
help prepare my manuscript for publi-
cation.

—Herbert Zincke,
October 1, 2002

I

Scott Field to Hawaii

April 7, 1937, to September 3, 1941

After my father died, my stepmother moved our family from Troy, New York, to St. Louis, Missouri. When I graduated from high school in 1937, the country was in the middle of the worst depression in its history. The only ready place to find a job even after finishing high school was the Army or Navy. So before I graduated, I enlisted in the Army Air Corps on April 7, 1937.

The sergeant at the Army recruiting office was receptive to my wish not to be stationed too far from home. He arranged duty for me at Scott Air Field—just eleven miles to the east across the Mississippi River into Illinois. Even so, it didn't turn out to be easy to get home on weekend leave. To start with, my basic pay of $21 per month—reduced to $17 by automatic debits—did not leave me with any money I could spend for transportation. Furthermore, the Air Field forbade hitchhiking, so I would just stand along the road a few blocks from the Air Field gate and, without sticking up my thumb, hope for the best. But soldiers and sailors weren't held in high regard in prewar America, so my passive hitching was not often successful. Of course, after the attack on Pearl Harbor, anyone in uniform didn't have to wait long to hitch a ride. But in 1937 I would get tired of standing in the cold and just trudge the eleven miles home, using the 19th century Eads bridge to cross the Mississippi into St. Louis.

Scott Air Field was mainly concerned with dirigibles and blimps, considered to be militarily useful for observation over enemy territory. But I was assigned to the maintenance squadron for the Air Field, so I had almost nothing to do with these craft. The very first thing they had me do was to polish brass door knobs in and around the office of the first sergeant of my squadron. His name was Ewald Davids, and he had reportedly been a German colonel in World War I. Now he was only a first sergeant but controlled all the enlisted men in the squadron.

As I was polishing a brass knob outside the sergeant's office, the base finance officer, a lieutenant colonel, entered the sergeant's office. I couldn't understand the conversation, but it soon increased in volume. Then the sergeant shouted, "I've been running this outfit for fifteen years, and I don't need any damn lieutenant colonel telling me how to do it!" The officer stalked out without a word. I was shocked and disgusted. Even as a recruit, I had respect for military discipline, and this was way off base.

I was a husky six-footer, weighing about 180 pounds, so they made me a military policeman. An early assignment was to guard work parties of Air Corps prisoners. As an MP, I was armed and had little trouble controlling my prisoners. Yet I was unsure what to do when a corporal on the base, who far outranked me as a private, demanded that I turn over one of my prisoners to him—presumably he had some job he wanted done. I had no instructions for such a case but uneasily complied with the corporal's request.

But at the end of the day I had to explain to the lieutenant at the MP office what had happened to the missing prisoner. He was furious and chewed me out, ending with, "Next time either bring back all your prisoners or shoot anyone who tries to take any!" This seemed extreme, but I said nothing. The guilty corporal was soon transferred and probably received a black mark on his service record.

The barber shop was across the hall from First Sergeant Davids' office. One day while I was waiting for a haircut, I noticed that the barber excused himself before finishing with the soldier in the chair—saying he had to go to the restroom. I could see through the door as the barber walked out. To my surprise, he slipped into Sgt. Davids' office instead of going to the restroom. He soon came back into the shop and finished the soldier's haircut. But the soldier had no sooner gotten out of the barber's chair than a corporal came in and assigned him to immediate latrine-cleaning duty.

While my hair was being cut, I tried to figure out what had happened. Then I recalled that the barber had been bending the ear of the soldier with typical service gripes, such as hinting that the first sergeant was diverting steaks and other goodies from the general mess. The soldier had responded by saying, "That must be so. No wonder our chow is so bad." After that, the barber had sneaked into the first sergeant's office—obviously to report the soldier's gripe about the food. The first sergeant had retaliated rapidly. In time, I found that the barber regularly served as a spy in this way for the first sergeant.

The first sergeant's diversion of steaks, chops, and fresh vegetables for himself and buddies was all too true. These goodies were consumed at parties at the sergeant's house on the base. On the other hand, our normal fare consisted of creamed chipped beef for breakfast and stew for dinner.

I finally received a little responsibility when a third class specialist transferred. He had been in charge of handling deliveries of gasoline to the air field. I saw that the gas was properly transferred to our tanks and kept track of the amount delivered. After doing this job for six months, I thought I deserved a promotion—it would mean a raise of $3 per month, but that was quite a raise when you were starting from $21.

All promotions had to go through First Sergeant Davids. First I had to go through channels for an appointment—even to talk with him. I was hoping for the best, since I had always been careful never to cross him. After I entered his office and saluted, he left me standing and barked, "What do you want?" I informed him I had been handling the delivery of gasoline to the base for the past six months—filling the slot for a third class specialist—and so was qualified for the promotion. The sergeant quickly answered, "Do you know where my house is and my car?" When I assured him I did, he went on, "Well, if you want to clean my quarters, wax my car, and mow the lawn this summer, I might be able to get you a promotion."

I stomped out of his office—so furious I decided then and there to get out of that place. But a transfer would involve the sergeant's consent, and I knew he would not approve. Just wanting someone to talk to, I confided in my friend, the Chief Clerk, who was a sergeant in another squadron on base. He listened carefully to my story and said he might be able to do something for me. I couldn't figure out what, but he told me next day, "If you wait until August, Sgt. Davids and his wife will be taking a month of leave at their cottage in the Ozarks of Missouri. I have been assigned to take the sergeant's place while he is on leave. Then we'll take care of you."

The first day of Davids' absence, the Chief Clerk did the paper work for my short discharge. I needed this to end my original enlistment early so as to make it possible for an overseas enlistment. I had been hearing about good duty overseas and was ready for more adventure than when I first enlisted. Now I had the choice of the Philippines or Hawaii. At first I leaned toward the Philippines because it was farther away. But an NCO with 30 years' service advised Hawaii because I would have less of a change in living conditions. He convinced me.

The paper work proceeded smoothly. When Ewald Davids returned, he accosted me outside his office, his face red with fury, and shouted,

"What do you mean by short-circuiting my authority?" I calmly replied, "You can't do anything about it, sergeant. The transfer papers have been approved through channels." There was nothing he could do except continue raving. Nor could he retaliate against the Chief Clerk, who was in another squadron on the base.

I had the choice of sailing from Brooklyn on the east coast or San Francisco on the west coast. I chose Brooklyn because my sister lived in New York. I had a fine time visiting her and going to the 1939 World's Fair. Then I sailed on a troop ship, the *Hunter Liggett*, but was lucky to have a bunk on "B" deck rather than in the hold, even though I was still a private. In watching our passage through the Panama Canal, I was fascinated by the locks and impressed by the engineering and construction of the canal.

At the Pacific end, we docked to refuel near Colon, the main city, and were let off the ship for a couple hours. Most of us headed for the Coconut Grove. Trying to keep up with my companions, I downed several giant-sized mugs of Panamanian beer, even though I wasn't used to drinking much beer. By the time I staggered back to the ship, I was bombed.

Our next stop was San Francisco. There it was so cold I had to dig out warmer clothes from my duffle bag. After a week of medical checks and paper work, we were glad to sail for the reported tropical paradise of Hawaii and its beautiful girls. A bus picked us up at the dock at Pearl Harbor and took us out to Schofield Barracks. I was indeed entranced by the tropical vegetation and the sunny, mild air as we passed the Royal Hawaiian Hotel on Waikiki Beach.

At first we bunked in four-man, wooden huts, and then I was assigned to a work party that was moving such huts from Luke Field on Ford Island to Hickam Field for the Air Corps soldiers soon to be stationed there. While working, I didn't realize that the corporal in charge of my work party was impressed with my work. I wouldn't know until after the war, when he was a lieutenant colonel and I was a warrant officer.

As soon as I had time off, I went down to Waikiki Beach to lie on the sand and listen to my portable radio. A couple of girls walked over to listen and maybe check me out. There was nothing worth listening to after awhile, so we had an enjoyable chat. After a time, one of them asked where I worked. But when I told them I was an Air Corps soldier at Hickam Field, they drifted away. Servicemen didn't seem to be held in any more esteem in Hawaii than in the U.S. Furthermore, the girls probably knew my pay as a soldier could be as low as $21 per month.

Nevertheless, I enjoyed serious swimming at the YMCA pool. It was some distance from the barracks, but I bought a Racer bicycle and used

B-17 Flying Fortress—our 14th Squadron was organized to fly this bomber and protect the Philippines with it. (National Air and Space Museum, SI Neg. No 95-9156)

it for frequent trips to the pool. It happened that the prevailing wind blew against me on the way; but after swimming, the wind boosted me back to Hickam Field with little pedaling needed.

I became a member of a bomb squadron that was training with twin-engined B-18s. We called the obsolete B-18 a "flying coffin," because if one engine went out, it was "curtains" for the pilot and crew. However, I happily took the on-board job of towing the target from the B-18 to provide firing practice for attacking aircraft. Once in flight I would let out the cloth target 1,000 behind feet on the tow line. After practice, and while still aloft, I let the cloth target go, reeled in the line, and attached metal "fish" that held and then released the target. The fish could not be used again, so when I had brought it back to the plane I would cut it off the line and let it drop.

One day I delayed cutting the fish until we were circling the field ready to land. Then I looked down and saw a lone soldier shaking his fist at us. After we landed, the same soldier, whom I recognized now, strode toward us—red-faced and furious. He shouted, "What are you trying to do, Zincke? Kill me? That fish missed my head by less than a foot and buried itself deep in the ground." I could only apologize, and he soon cooled off. No one reported the incident, so it was a cheap lesson for me.

Such close calls tended to be ignored during the Air Corps build-up at Hickam Field—war was expected. As more men arrived, I became an old-timer and worked hard and successfully for promotion to a corporal. Then in 1940, after the shiny, new, four-engined Flying Fortresses (B-17s) flew in, I was assigned as the armorer-gunner on the flight crew of a particular B-17.

I had the responsibility for loading the plane with bombs and ammunition, and then going aloft as a gunner on bombing missions. I liked the job and the extra flight pay. In the summer of 1941 we became members of the provisional 14th Bomb Squadron—being formed at Hickam Field to fly seven or eight of the new B-17 bombers. The 14th had been given a secret mission. But it wasn't secret for long—we were going to the Philippines.

II

Clark Field, Philippines

September 3, 1941, to December 24, 1941

On September 3, 1941, I boarded the troop ship *President Pierce* at Honolulu and sailed for the Philippines. I had just been promoted to staff sergeant in the 14th Bomb Squadron of the Army Air Corps. That summer I had used a 30-day leave to visit the nearby island of Hawaii, where I spent most of my time while enjoying the company of a cute Portuguese-Filipina girl.

Now we sailed west from Honolulu for two days without escort before the USS *Houston*, a light cruiser, appeared and stayed with us most of the way as we sailed a zigzag course to foil torpedo attacks, even though the U.S. was not at war. In addition, we observed a strict blackout. The Far East situation had become more tense after July 25, 1941, when Japanese troops landed in Indo-China, now Viet Nam. The same day, President Roosevelt embargoed U.S. exports of scrap iron and oil to Japan—crucial to Japan's continuing war against China.

On the *President Pierce*, the 200 or so men of my 14th Squadron slept on "B" deck, the first deck below the main deck. We fared much better than the 200th Coast Artillery from New Mexico, who slept and ate in the hold—they had boarded in San Francisco. My promotion to staff sergeant now paid off in an unexpected way—I ate with the second sitting in the officers' dining hall and was served the same menu.

On September 15 we docked in Manila, where we boarded Army buses that took us 60 miles north to Clark Air Field. It was the largest air base in the Philippines, but had grass runways. The next morning at breakfast we noticed small, black men, naked except for GI T-shirts, hanging around

9

the garbage cans outside. After breakfast we dumped our trays where the little men stood, waiting to dive in for leftovers. We soon learned they were called Negritos—we thought they were about four feet tall. They had the run of the base because General Arthur MacArthur, father of Douglas, had agreed to share the use of the area with them in 1898—five years before the Wright brothers' first flight.

A few days later, the ten B-17 bombers (Flying Fortresses) of our 14th Squadron arrived from Hawaii. We were immediately put on "alert" for any emergency. At the same time, we began to install armor plates behind the pilot and co-pilot seats. It was difficult to raise and install the plates without winches or mechanical assists, and the heat trapped inside the bomber was fierce. It took me two days to finish my plane, but I was proud of the result.

My regular duty was to load bombs and ammunition on one B-17 and to oversee the loading of three other B-17s. I liked the job, and in Hawaii had been pleased with the 10 percent bonus for flight pay. At Clark Field I had the same task of getting the bombers loaded, but my job as the armorer no longer included being a gunner on the flight crew—the result, no more flight pay. I was not happy about this.

On October 23, more B-17 bombers reached Clark Field—they came from March Field, California. Those bombers and our 14th Bomb Squadron made up the 19th Bomb Group. There were now 35 B-17s in the Philippines, all based at Clark Field. But on December 5, our 14th Squadron commander, Major Emmet (Rosie) O'Donnell, took 17 of the B-17s, including the 14th Squadron bombers, 400 miles south to Del Monte Air Field. There, on the large southern island of Mindanao, the bombers were well beyond the range of Japanese bombers based on Formosa. Yet the B-17s still at Clark remained within easy range of air attack—Formosa lay just 300 miles to the north.

Early on the morning of December 8, we heard the first radio reports of the Japanese attack on Pearl Harbor. Later in the morning our B-17s at Clark took off, cruising aimlessly to save them from being caught on the ground by a Japanese attack. But they returned at 11:30 A.M. to refuel— they had finally been ordered to bomb Formosa. At noon the bombers were still being serviced and the crews were eating lunch when we sighted a large formation of approaching aircraft. Since they looked like large U.S. Navy planes, we just stood there and counted 54 of them. But then someone yelled, "Navy, hell! Those are Japs!" We all ran through the hangar, and the guys with me piled into some prepared foxholes. But something told me not to jump in there. Instead I sprinted to a large trench a hundred yards farther. As I leaped in, I remember seeing the first bomb hit our hangar. I felt surprisingly calm and stood in the trench watching the bombs drop for an indeterminable period of a minute or two—maybe shorter.

Then I noticed that after the bombs exploded, white smoke billowed up with a hissing. All I could think of was poison gas. I yanked off my $20 prescription sunglasses, slapped on my gas mask, and dug into the bottom of the foxhole like a mole. It was a darn good thing that it wasn't gas, because I got the "flutter valve" of the mask full of dirt and nearly suffocated trying to breathe. I laugh at myself now, but I thought then that I'd had it.

Finally the explosions stopped and the sound of the bombers' engines faded. I raised my head just far enough for a quick glance toward our B-17s—they had been parked in a row ready to take off. But now I could see no intact B-17 among the wreckage of our once beautiful aircraft. Then through the smoke and fire I noticed men running and yelling in pain and shock, so I knew there was no danger of gas. I threw off my mask and ran toward the wrecked aircraft—even though I didn't know what I could do to help. But then I heard machine gun fire and the scream of diving aircraft—enemy fighter planes had come to strafe us after the bombers had done their work.

I doubled back and ran through our barracks and past some foxholes, but I didn't jump in. Then I must have broken all existing track records while searching for another foxhole, but could find none. Finally, I spotted men diving into a long, straight drainage ditch. I leaped in and landed on top of a mass of humanity that was wriggling like worms, trying to burrow deeper. I managed to squirm under at least one or two bodies.

The Japanese fighters whined overhead while the steady fire of machine guns and intermittent thud of 20 mm shells made our blood run cold. We all realized our desperately thin chance of surviving if a Jap plane should spot us. Because our ditch was straight and open, it would have been a massacre if one enemy plane started firing at one end and flew to the other—one pass would kill or wound 100 men.

We were absolutely helpless. Many men lost their nerve and tried to get up to run away from the death trap. But there was a lieutenant in with us who had sense enough to quiet the near panic by commanding, loudly enough for all to hear, "Everyone remain absolutely still. I'll shoot the first man who raises his head!" At the same time, he waved his .45 automatic gun to prove he meant it. I could feel the tenseness go out of the bodies of the men crunched against me, and silence reigned supreme. But I still feared that one of the very young boys might lose his nerve and make a break and run. My heart kept beating rapidly until, after what seemed an eternity, the last Jap fighter whined away toward Manila. It was determined later that the strafing part of the enemy attack had lasted about 35 minutes, while the bombing part had lasted about 18 minutes.

After crawling out of the ditch, I went back to look for my expensive sunglasses. I couldn't find them, but that loss was nothing compared to our human casualties—at Clark there were 93 dead and 143 wounded. The foxholes I had run past when the raid began were the center of a terrible mess. Parts of bodies were strewn about to a radius of 50 feet—apparently the result of a direct hit. What had made me keep running instead of jumping in there—to certain death? This was the first of many times during the war when I have wondered why the Grim Reaper didn't sweep me along with others who were less fortunate.

All but two of our 17 shiny new bombers had been destroyed. It saddened me to see those beautiful bombers I had worked on with such care lying torn and broken. Many were now merely molten heaps, recognizable only by the four engines smoldering in front of an outline of charred and melted metal. I could not have imagined such a tragedy—half the bomber strength of the Philippines was eliminated in half an hour.

After helping the medics clean up the debris of shattered and unidentified bodies, I reported to the 14th Squadron area, which was virtually untouched. But our barracks were visible from the air, so we packed up our personal belongings and moved to Margot, a tiny village on the edge of the airfield. Its trees offered overhead cover against the air raids sure to come. There we dug foxholes. I used the armor plating from the destroyed B-17s to line my foxhole, and others did the same.

The B-17s that had been withdrawn to Del Monte Air Field before the Japanese attack began to operate against the enemy—stopping at Clark for bombs and servicing. Since the raid, bulldozers had filled many of the craters on the runways. Every evening at dusk a few B-17s from Del Monte would carefully land and apply brakes on the uneven grass runways. Then we hauled the bombers into the cover of the jungle to service them and load the bombs.

One of the B-17 bombers lost on these missions had particular significance for me—I had been the armourer-gunner on its flight crew during training in Hawaii. But after the Air Corps split this job in two, I was unhappily left on the ground as armourer—without flight pay—while a new man replaced me as the flight gunner. But the Air Corps decision had almost surely saved my life. During the night, we brought out .50 cal. ammunition and the 600-pound bombs. It usually required three men to load each bomb. Because of my size (6 ft. and 180 lbs.), I usually lifted at the middle of the bomb while two others helped at the ends—usually members of the flight crew. They needed us to load the bombs, but most of them didn't want us to fool around with their guns—I didn't blame them. We worked very hard to keep this skeleton of an air force in operating condition so we could blast those damn Japs like they blasted us.

Early on the morning of December 10 we were loading 600-pounders when Col. Ewbanks, our 19th Group Commander, swerved out on the runway in his staff car and yelled for us to clear the field—we had only ten minutes before an air raid. My loading crew had loaded three bombs on our ship, and a fourth was ready on the sling, when the combat crew scrambled to their places. As the engines roared, we barely managed to drop the fourth bomb on the ground before our ship headed for the runway with its bomb bay doors open and its bomb slings flapping.

Many men have claimed the honor of loading the three famous bombs on Colin Kelly's ship that day, but I know it was Sgt. Warren R. Stewart, Jr., who had been assigned to Kelly's ship and never let anyone else do his loading. This was Kelly's last flight, but it made him famous. He flew north at 30,000 feet to Aparri on the northern tip of Luzon, where the crew spotted a large convoy coming toward the coast. Captain Kelly picked out the largest ship in the convoy, and Mike Levin, the bombardier, dropped all of his three bombs toward the target. He scored two direct hits and one near miss, leaving the ship burning and listing badly.*

Now Jap fighters showed up, so Kelly headed back to Clark—he had no bombs left anyway. When he lowered down to his final leg, a Jap fighter—some said two fighters—jumped him. On the first burst, Staff Sgt. Delehanty, engineer, was killed with a 20 mm shell through the head. On the second pass, the enemy hit the oxygen line and the ship burst into flames. The crew bailed out except for the pilot, co-pilot, and navigator. Those who bailed out reported that the Japs strafed them all the way down. Fortunately, they were not injured, but Staff Sgt. Halkyard, assistant engineer, showed me many bullet holes in his flying suit.

The co-pilot, Lt. Donald Robbins, tried to get out through the bombardier's escape hatch, but the door had stuck. With the flames getting close, he just sat down on the step from the pilot's compartment to his station and said, "To hell with it." But he had picked the right spot to sit down. The next thing he knew, the bomber blew up around him and left him sitting in space, still conscious. So he pulled his ripcord and floated

*The U.S. press reported that Captain Colin Kelly had steered his burning bomber into the Japanese battleship Haruna and left it sinking. But since the war, the ship has been determined to have been the cruiser Ashigara, which survived the attack and operated until the war ended.

down, seriously burned but still alive. Robbins told his story to some of the boys who visited him in the hospital in Manila. Nobody knows why Captain Kelly's chute did not open, but most of us believed that he went out the overhead escape hatch and knocked himself unconscious on the vertical stabilizer.

The enemy aircraft did attack Clark that morning, as Col. Ewbanks had warned, but the B-17s had left just in time. Then there was nothing to bomb but the runways—the buildings had already been destroyed. After the enemy flew off, we hurried to fill up the craters so B-17s from Del Monte Field could land that evening.

There had been fires on Mt. Arayat, about five miles east of us, the night before this raid. The fires were arranged to point toward Clark Field—fifth columnists had lit them every night for a week. Finally I noticed a company of fully-armed Philippine Scouts of the 26th Division heading for Mt. Arayat—the 26th was stationed at Ft. Stotsenburg, which adjoined Clark Field. I never learned how many traitors the Scouts had caught, but the fires ceased. We sent up a prayer of thanks to the Scouts.

The 14th Squadron moved to the cover of a large banana grove on the northwest side of the runways on December 12. We were still loading B-17s coming up from Del Monte every evening to bomb the invading Japanese. But fewer of them survived their missions against the enemy—leaving us with less and less to do.

At 0200 on December 22, the 14th Squadron was aroused and deployed near the bomb dump. The other men and officers at Clark were stationed to complete a ring around the field. About a half dozen light tanks and half-tracks were stationed where they could easily be seen—more for the sake of morale than defense against a full-scale landing supported by strafing fighters. It would have been a slaughter, but we would have gotten a lot of them before they hit this spot of American soil. It wasn't until nearly dawn that officers informed us that they expected a parachute invasion—as if we hadn't figured that out. By 0800, however, base authorities no longer expected an immediate attack. They ordered the 14th Squadron and other outfits back to their bivouac areas—the 14th doubled its regular guard.

After dark on Christmas Eve, the 14th Squadron and the rest of the 19th Bomb Group boarded trucks and headed south for Bataan peninsula, while some members of the 440th Aviation Ordnance stayed behind to blow up the bomb dump. We were a few miles on our way, groping through the dark outside San Fernando, when sparks and dull explosions to our rear told us the ordnance boys were doing their job.

Staff Sgt. Jimmy Palmer, out mess sergeant, had managed to cook us a fine Christmas dinner during the day, but we had to take it all with us to eat after we bivouacked. Palmer was from St. Louis, and he worked like hell getting us good food. Because of Palmer, our squadron ate good, wholesome chow, and lots of it, when other squadrons were relying on local rice for their basic fare.

III

Bataan to Malabang

December 24, 1941, to April 20, 1942

We rode our trucks all night before making camp on Christmas Day in the wild jungle near the south coast of the peninsula of Bataan. The trees, thick brush, and vines made it look like a difficult place for an enemy to invade.

We could see the island of Corregidor and watch the Japanese bombers cautiously feeling out the strength of this great fortress. The Nips would come over in "V" formation, usually nine to a flight, but our heavy antiaircraft fire dispersed the bombers before they could drop any bombs on their target. More than a dozen enemy aircraft found a watery grave in Manila Bay in the few days we were there.

Our Navy PT boats were forever patrolling the bay and idly cruising at a distance from shore—they were hoping to lure Japanese pursuit planes to come after them. When a "sucker" did dive down to strafe, the PT boat kicked its three Packard engines into high gear and skimmed the water in an erratic pattern, with the enemy fighter hot on its trail. God, what courage those men had! With practically no armor protection, they relied on their boats' speed and maneuverability, and their gunners' accuracy. I saw more than one enemy pilot learn respect for these PT boats too late, falling victim to the fire of the brace of .50 caliber guns each boat carried.

On December 29, however, the enemy bombers made a more concerted effort on Corregidor at a much higher altitude. At 30,000 feet, they were out of range of the outdated antiaircraft guns the 200th and 60th Coast Artillery were firing—their shells burst into black puffs far below the bombers. The enemy scored many hits on the top of Corregidor, but we could not tell how much damage they did because smoke blocked out our view. But flames leaping above the smoke showed Corregidor's location. A few enemy planes were hit and crashed into land or the sea. Still, wave after wave loosed their destruction on the island. Heretofore, it had been known as the "Invincible Fortress," but now our boys were up against serious odds.

On Bataan, watching, we were safe except for the rain of fiery pieces of metal that fell from the sky—shrapnel from the Coast Artillery anti-aircraft guns. At first, when I'd hear the falling shrapnel's scream, I would "hit the dirt," but then I figured a greater area of me was exposed that way. So I stood straight up and tried to figure out from the sound if it was coming my way. Finally, I just ignored the chunks of metal, since it was impossible to tell if one would land on my head or a mile away. I did wear my helmet for protection, but if a piece had hit my tin hat, it would have gone clear through it and me—so what the hell! That night our squadron moved again—hoping for a safer location. But before long, shrapnel was shattering trees and limbs all around us.

That night we broke camp, boarded trucks, and headed for the port of Mariveles. What a wild ride that was—on steep, narrow roads that a mountain goat would be a fool to try climbing! Yet these steel-nerved Marine Corps drivers kept the two-ton Federals at top speed. Why we never landed at the bottom of a thousand-foot ravine, and how we managed to stay on the right road, driving in a full blackout, I'll never know! But we arrived at Mariveles just as dawn was breaking.

The inter-island steamer *Mayon* was waiting at the dock. We loaded all our equipment aboard and then were told to come back at 9 P.M. Meantime, we wandered around town—not a Japanese bombing target at that time. Most stores and the movie theaters were closed. But a few cabarets were still open—it had been a real servicemen's town.

When we reached the dock that night, there was a mass of men and vehicles crowded into a small area. It seemed like we were in terrible danger from an air attack. Yet the Japs were not flying at night. Some of the Fourth Marine Division out of China were trying to direct traffic. In the confusion they herded us like cattle to the *Mayon*. A nearby explosion scared us but did not interrupt boarding. The 14th Squadron and other squadrons of the 19th Group crowded the ship with 600 Air Corps soldiers, except for a few radiomen transferred to an infantry outfit, who stayed behind. Our ship slipped away from the dock and moved through the black waters. We could just make out the massive dark shape of Corregidor. But suddenly a blinding searchlight challenged us from the island. The *Mayon* flashed back its identity, and then we were flashed directions that guided us through the island's minefields. We soon were following the coast of Luzon southward, steaming as fast as our small ship could go, and always keeping in sight of land.

At dawn we pulled into a beautiful, jungle-enclosed cove at a small island off the coast of the larger island of Romblon. It seemed like a good place to wait until nightfall, when it would be safe to proceed. But at 2 P.M. a Japanese flying boat, looking like our Navy PBY, flew overhead. It went by while we held our breath and stayed stretched out under a tarpaulin we had rigged to protect us from the sun. Then, when we thought we were safe, the enemy plane circled back and came down to look us over. We were too large for a fishing craft and obviously trying to hide, so the slow, clumsy aircraft began to drop its six 100-pound bombs—one at a time and from a low altitude, since we had no anti-aircraft guns. We sat there helplessly while that damn patrol bomber dropped one bomb on each run—wondering why they didn't blow us to Kingdom Come. We were the ultimate "sitting ducks."

After the fourth bomb, I wiggled over to the hatch cover and lowered myself into the small hold and crawled beside some boxes for protection. Although I wasn't really safer there than on deck, I felt better not having to possibly watch a bomb drop on my lap. While I was there, a bomb dropped so close to the ship that the explosion tore a hole in the hull of the *Mayon* near the waterline. Inside the hold, I was tumbled against a bulkhead by the rocking ship, but the heavy boxes did not move. Stunned and frightened, I didn't stir. But when some time passed without another explosion, I crawled to the hatch and raised it. The sunlight poured into the hold on the label of one of the heavy boxes. I read, "Warning! TNT! Handle with Care." I scrambled out on the main deck and was ready to jump overboard until I noticed the Filipino Captain standing in a swirl of black smoke with a half-smile on his face. Still, again the bomber came back and made another pass over the stricken *Mayon*, but without dropping another bomb. Then it lumbered off for good. The Captain's smile became a chuckle. He had thrown up the cloud of black smoke to make the enemy believe the *Mayon* was finished.

During the raid, some of our men lost their nerve and jumped over the side—contrary to Major O'Donnell's orders not to jump into the water. Some couldn't swim well enough to cope with the strong current and were being carried out to sea. Victor Mapes, a 14th Squadron cook, admitted that he was one of the first to dive off the ship, and he passed by a number of floundering Americans on his way to the beach. But as he climbed out of the water, Mapes noticed a fisherman standing by a canoe. Mapes, a vigorous-looking cook, persuaded the Filipino to paddle

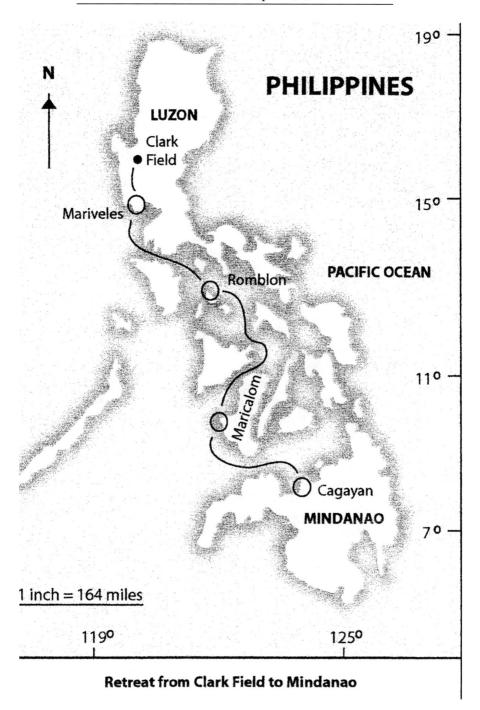

Retreat from Clark Field to Mindanao

him out to the faltering Americans. Mapes and the Filipino rescued seven GIs.*

As soon as the raider was out of sight, we Americans still aboard hurried to get ashore by lifeboat or by swimming. I swam the short distance, enjoying the cool and refreshing water. We scrambled up the sand beach to the shelter of coconut palms—we still expected the Japs to come back. But they were probably so ashamed of their bombing that they didn't dare report to their superiors that they had dropped six bombs on a defenseless ship at a low altitude and couldn't sink it or even score a hit. But we were still greatly relieved when dusk came without a sign of the enemy. Somewhat miraculously, the *Mayon* not only rode high in the water but was ready to sail—the Filipino captain and crew had stayed aboard and pumped and then patched the hole at the waterline.

When we reboarded, my small friend, Dick Beck of the 14th Squadron, became delirious because he thought the *Mayon* was still under attack. He was still suffering from a concussion that resulted when one of the Japanese bombs exploded close to him while he was swimming ashore. The *Mayon* was already underway on its southward journey before we were able to coax Dick below deck and to the sick bay, where medics eventually calmed him down. Others in the water had close calls, but no other casualties from the bombs resulted.

After a quiet, all-night voyage, we pulled into a cove on the southwestern coast of Negros Island at dawn. But we did not feel very secure after our experience in a similar cove the day before. We were stunned, though, when full daylight revealed a ship lying on the bottom almost directly under us. Then we noticed life preservers and some debris floating near the shore of the cove. Nobody wanted to stay on the ship, so we spent the rest of the day on shore, but this time no enemy aircraft found the *Mayon*. On land we learned that the ship lying on the bottom was the inter-island passenger ship, the *Panay*, a sister ship of our *Mayon*, and the same size. It had been sunk the day before and was carrying arms for our forces on Negros. The crew had escaped, but the captain had gone down with his ship. In the evening we boarded again and headed across open water for the island of Mindanao.

At mid-morning on January 1, 1942, we docked at Cagayan on the north coast of Mindanao—the southernmost Philippine island and the largest after Luzon. Everything looked peaceful to us, but Major O'Donnell gave the order to "load and lock," and to disperse as soon as we hit shore—no one knew if the enemy was near or not. But no Japs were in

*See Victor L. Mapes, The Butchers, the Baker *(McFarland, 2000), pages 39–40.*

sight, and the Filipinos said they had not seen any as yet. We set up camp in a coconut grove while our officers left for Del Monte Air Field to obtain orders. Del Monte Field was only ten miles away—it was where O'Donnell had taken half the B-17s before the war began, to get them out of range of Japanese bombers based on Formosa.

I knew I would need a bolo after I noticed the heavy jungle. Bolos are long, sturdy knives used by the Filipinos to harvest crops and cut brush. I paid the high price of five pesos—about $2.50 in prewar U.S. money. Mine was strong and heavy-bladed, with its handle carved in the shape of an alligator's head. It served me well—it would cut through any brush and small trees.

The second day after landing at Cagayan, the 14th Squadron camped along the road to Del Monte Air Field and posted guards. Here we learned to make beds for ourselves—in doing so I found immediate use for my bolo. First we cut down small trees to make four posts, each four-feet long and with a diameter of three inches. They formed the corners of the bed—one end of each post was sharpened and driven in the ground, leaving the chosen natural fork on top. Then the bed was finished with smaller branches and lots of vine. The beds were fairly comfortable, but the vines had to be tightened or replaced by morning. Every night we carefully smeared oil or grease on each post to thwart visits by spiders, scorpions, and centipedes.

We made a night move to the vicinity of Del Monte Field on January 8. It was dark when we arrived, so we just stretched out on the ground along the road instead of making camp. When the sound of aircraft awoke us in bright daylight, we were horrified to see how exposed we were to enemy strafing. The aircraft turned out to be friendly, but we quickly moved back from the road to the shelter of a 500-yard-long, narrow grove of small trees. Behind was an open field, and across the road the dense growth of the Del Monte pineapple plantation provided no space for camping. We were supposed to camp under these small trees—we called this campsite the "Suicide Strip" and stayed carefully hidden under the scanty cover. The mess crew rubbed sand on all of their shiny pots and pans so they would not glint in the sun. Our luck was stretching to the limit, but we spent a very quiet time there—not complaining much when it rained like the devil and we had to sleep one night in muddy foxholes—we didn't even consider cutting down trees to make beds there.

Only a few American planes used Del Monte Air Field. One was a P-40 fighter flown by Lt. Brown. He flew up to Luzon and back with messages, and occasionally shot down or chased enemy aircraft that challenged him. One evening after Lt. Brown had landed and taxied into a hiding place, a Jap plane winged slowly back and forth over Del Monte Field for a time before turning away into a cloud cover. But in five minutes the Jap emerged from the clouds and headed our way—this time with a companion. Lt. Brown, however, had not fallen for the scheme. The Jap pilot had hoped his apparent departure would entice Brown to get into the air and face the danger of being shot down before he could reach fighting altitude. Instead, Brown just stood in the brush while the two enemy aircraft made another search. Then he grinned as they flew away. We watched the game from Suicide Strip with fascination and then glee.

We felt still more uneasy when flares in the mountains made us fear that fifth columnists would report our location. But B-17 operations in the Philippines were ending, so the Air Corps had to figure out what to do with us. We were overjoyed when orders came for the 14th Squadron to pack 14 days' rations for a trek into northwest Mindanao. There, near Lake Lanao (and hopefully far from enemy air attack), the 14th Squadron had a secret assignment. We would make our last stand there and hold out—if possible—until aid arrived from the U.S. Furthermore, the lake was full of fish and ducks, and vegetables and fruit thrived in the cooler climate—the altitude of the lake was 2100 feet. We eagerly loaded our trucks and could hardly wait for darkness—the only safe time to leave Suicide Strip.

We retraced the dark mountain road downward toward Cagayan very slowly, remembering the steep slopes that dropped from the roadside to deep ravines below. After daylight we kept moving, but had to drive the trucks off the road several times when we heard enemy planes. We turned west at Cagayan and followed the coast along a road bordered by coconut trees. A few villages and groups of huts lined the beach, where fish nets and outrigger canoes lay unattended except for an occasional lonely figure.

Then in the jungle again, we noticed monkeys, a wild boar, and lizard-like creatures that turned out to be iguanas. Most striking, though, was a man who strode along the road like he owned it. At his hip hung a kris, a sword with a wavy, double-edged blade, and over his shoulder a shotgun. He wore a dark-green, silk shirt and tight-legged pants. His head was topped with a fez and tassel. He was chewing something that smeared his mouth and lips with red stain. We later learned that he was a Moro who was chewing betel nut, a mild narcotic. (The Moros had settled on Mindanao centuries before the arrival of the Spanish in the 16th century. Thereafter they had resisted all Spanish attempts to subdue them and retained their Islam religion—nor had American rule since 1900 changed the Moros' independent way of life.)

Farther on, the houses and gardens were neater and looked more prosperous. We noticed several women with raven-black hair loosely knotted behind the head, and men in large straw hats like those worn by Chinese coolies.

On the evening of January 16 we stopped at Iligan, a port on Iligan Bay. An American infantry officer asked where we had come from. After absorbing the story of our retreat from Clark Field and Bataan, he told us his troops had seen little action. But they had covered many roofs in town, including the church's tin roof, with palm fronds, and they had dug foxholes and stacked sandbags around gun emplacements. We stayed all night at Iligan, so there was time for the boys to shop, but they found nothing except cheap gin.

The next morning we turned south away from the coast. Most of the day our convoy climbed steadily over winding mountain roads through dense jungle. By late afternoon we reached open country and soon drove into Momungan, a small town surrounded by fields of corn, beans, and sweet potatoes, as well as pastures where cattle and carabao (water buffalo used as work animals) grazed. At the edge of town stood a good-sized open-air market.

At the market Filipino soldiers greeted us, as well as some Moros who wanted to trade. Our men bought knives and swords—the largest weapon was an old two-handed sword that one of our truck drivers bought at a high price. He made quite a spectacle with the old relic—it was taller than he was. Also at the market were ears of boiled corn that cost very little—a real treat, since we hadn't had fresh corn since leaving the U.S. Our appetite amazed the bystanders.

We returned to our trucks and climbed higher into the mountain. Along the way we wondered about a steady roar that seemed to be coming out of the jungle ahead. It became louder until we came to an opening and gazed at a spectacular waterfall that thundered into the river beside the road. It was the Maria Cristina Falls on the Agus River, which flows northward out of Lake Lanao and carries its water from an altitude of 2100 feet to sea level near Iligan. We ascended onward through lush rain forest toward the lake. It was almost dark when we camped near Lake Lanao.

On the morning of January 18 our convoy passed through a town of attractive buildings that shone in the sunlight. It was Dansalan, a provincial capital, which bordered Lake Lanao and the Agus River. There was no sign of bomb damage. We noticed a general cheerfulness on the faces of the Filipinos who watched us go by. Then we realized that the people took us to be reinforcements from the U.S. Continuing a mile or less through town, we saw the modern barracks of Camp Keithley across

Top: Camp Keithley—Filipino troops were driven out by Japanese air attack; It was later used to hold American and Filipino POWs. (National Archives, SC 315919) *Left:* Bridge over Agus River, four miles north of Lake Lanao—the Agus flows north from lake to sea near Iligan. (Photograph by J.D. Givens, courtesy Jane Frederickson)

the river—our destination. At Keithley a lone Filipino officer greeted us and explained that Camp Keithley had been evacuated by the Philippine Scouts after a Japanese bombing attack on December 20. The Scouts had not come back because of Japanese control of the air; the Jap bombers had flown low over Dansalan and dropped leaflets saying their forces would take over, and that no harm would come to the people if they behaved themselves. The Filipino officer told us that thousands of Moros were willing to fight the Japs. Yet their weapons were limited to home-made water pipe rifles and bolos.

When our men discovered that the showers in the abandoned barracks were still working, we rushed to use them. While we were enjoying this luxury, someone yelled, "Take Cover." We dashed out to look for planes but found none. But the false alarm certainly sobered us up. Then, in finding spaces to bunk, the debris of cement, sheet iron, and glass spooked us, even though wreckage was not new to us—some were ready to leave right then.

After chow, the officers announced that all but 30 of us were moving the next day. But that was not very relaxing, because we didn't know which 30 had to stay. The next morning Sgt. Scott called out the names of the 30 who were not going, and the rest of us said goodbye to our buddies, not knowing if we would see them again. I was glad to be among those leaving the wreckage of Camp Keithley.

Driving south along the western shore of the lake, we drank in the natural beauty and breathed the cool morning air. We passed Moro farmyards full of chickens and sometimes a goat or caribou. Women in brightly colored sarongs stared sleepily from doorways. Several Jap bombers forced us off the road. Then we hastily covered our trucks with leafy branches and scattered to separate cover in case the trucks were found. We had to do this more than once before we reached the large Moro village of Genassi at the south end of Lake Lanao.

Here Jap bombers were again overhead—we drove under bamboo trees and spread out in the pastures and gardens around the village. Above the roar of planes we heard the ominous sound of gongs, which brought Moro warriors with shotguns and knives running toward us. Were the gongs urging attack against us or simply warning the Moros of the Jap aircraft? When the Moros suddenly dived into nearby ditches and brush, we realized they were in the same boat with us. But there was no attack, and the planes flew off.

Then we assembled at the edge of Genassi to receive directions from Captain Lane, who had lived in the region. After leaving him, we continued southward barely a mile when Jap planes came looking for a target. But they could not find us under the heavy jungle growth where we had driven. But we scattered away from the trucks anyway. Then we headed upward on a winding mountain road. After passing a few villages and crossing several streams, we entered an uninhabited region of small lakes surrounded by steep mountain walls.

In late afternoon we descended to a town on flat land, from where coconut plantations stretched into the distance. After passing through the town, we looked for cover where we could wait for orders in relative safety. After all the planes that had been looking for us, we hated to be on open ground in the daytime.

The only spot we could find didn't look good, even after we hurriedly covered the trucks with palm leaves. We sought cover for ourselves in thin underbrush that was some distance from the trucks, hot and anxious to get going. We sat in the scant shade, sweating it out. But our luck held. We were there only an hour before our orders came. In a couple of miles we reached Malabang, passed through it, and entered dense jungle. We came to a turnoff that quickly brought us to a small opening in the jungle, harboring a few crude shacks.

Huge tropical trees with large twisting vines and dense foliage prevented sunlight from reaching the ground. This shadowy place did not depress us—we would be hard to see from the air. Captain William Horrigan, a pilot, gave instructions on how to build a camp. He was a large-framed, easygoing officer who had been in the Philippines for several years. His warnings not to cut down any heavy foliage or congregate on the road were not necessary. Then Major Luther Heidger, a flight surgeon from the 19th Bomb Group, called us together—he had just joined us. He stressed the need for strict sanitary measures because our hideout was near sea level and very humid—conditions conducive to breeding tropical diseases. He was persuasive because of his direct manner and beaming smile. His mood rubbed off on us, and we felt better after hiding from Jap planes all day.

We were here to maintain a small airfield nearby—we were to keep it in readiness for the dreamed-of arrival of aircraft from Australia. We had hundreds of barrels of high-octane gas, oil, and a large bomb dump, which the 701st Ordnance unit maintained. But no aircraft flew in to be serviced in the first days we were there, and we doubted any would come.

Our jungle surroundings were enchanting—in particular, an ice-cold, crystal clean spring bubbled out of the rocks in the middle of our clearing. It filled a natural basin in which two of us could bathe at once. The overflow from our bathtub trickled down a series of rocks to a winding stream that flowed into the Matling River, a short distance away.

Directly above the spring, a large patch of blue sky could be seen—surrounded by the dark canopy of the jungle. A simple bamboo hut with a palm-thatched roof stood by the spring and was reflected in the pool of water. A sign announced something in Arabic writing. We learned that the writing had to do with the Islamic faith. In fact, during sacred days of the Islam calendar, Moros came from miles around to bathe in the spring's basin and pray to Allah inside the sacred hut. Animal tracks in the moist sand by the pool showed that jungle creatures also used the spring. Because of the place's religious significance, we kept the pool clean and stayed away from the ceremonial hut. We sensed our good fortune to be safely hidden there. But the men began to gripe about having only two meals a day, usually consisting of rice and hash.

As directed by Major Heidger, the men dug a latrine and garbage pit, and then paired off to build two-man shelters for sleeping. To fend off mosquitoes, we used tattered mosquito nets. Captain Horrigan and Major Heidger hired some Moros to build shelters for a hospital and kitchen. The Moros wielded bolos to cut vines, poles, and palm leaves to build the sturdy shacks.

The first day we used the new kitchen, Palmer and Mapes fixed hash, sweet potatoes, and coffee for us. Captain Horrigan had just stood up for an announcement when the roar of planes destroyed our brief sense of security there. After the planes flew on, Horrigan told us that we would be the maintenance crew at the nearby airstrip.

One evening we were startled by a roar of a motor—not in the air but on the ground. Soon John Murdock of our 14th Squadron burst into our hideout on a motorcycle. We had not seen him since we left Del Monte Air Field. He had been able to transfer to the Air Corps unit there, but had changed his mind and wanted to come back with us. Now he groaned, "I ache all over … Jesus, I think I'm going to break into pieces, I rode that god damn motorcycle all the way from Del Monte, and them damn slant-eyes kept trying to send me to hell. I was bombed and strafed … but I just rubbed my lucky leg, picked myself off the road, and here I am." But Murdock was still shaky the next morning when a low-flying enemy plane awakened us soon after sunrise.*

The airstrip we were supposed to maintain required a lot of work because Jap planes kept coming over and dropping bombs, causing craters that had to be filled up—we had a small bulldozer to do this. And the repairs kept bringing more attacks.

But it was still boring to be in our hideout after the day's work. So after the sun had set, the men took off in our old truck to enjoy the nightlife of the small town of Malabang. We felt safe for the evening because the Japs did not fly after dark. On the way we passed bamboo shacks, thatched with palm leaves, which had yards with pigs, chickens, and dogs. Farther on, we drove by better houses, which had no pigs about—an almost sure sign that Moros lived there, faithful to their Islam religion. Next we passed ancient-looking fortifications, which the Spanish had built long ago to defend against the fierce Moros. There had been intermittent armed

*Mapes, The Butchers, the Baker, *page 54.*

struggles between the Catholic Spaniards and Islamic Moros during Spanish rule of the Philippines that lasted from the 16th century until the Spanish War of 1898, when Spain lost the Philippines to the U.S.

We finally reached the town's hotel, which had a bar that was the extent of the town's nightlife. Here we could buy cheap drinks, boiled eggs, and coffee, as well as tuba, the favorite Philippine alcoholic drink, made from coconuts.

One evening Bill Knortz didn't stop at the hotel bar but continued down to the Matling River. There, he told us, he had watched Captain Charles Wyatt load homemade depth charges on a motor boat and head down the river toward the Moro Gulf. Wyatt was an engineering officer in the Philippine 81st Division, which was stationed near Malabang. Knortz told us he had learned that Wyatt hoped to drop depth charges on the Japanese submarine that was thought to be lurking nearby, coming up at night to send fifth column messages. Wyatt was in ragged clothes, hoping to look like a Filipino fisherman, but his large athletic build and wavy red hair didn't help the disguise. Knortz ended his account of Wyatt with, "Boy, I wish I was with him. What an adventure." Knortz did go out on the same hunt with Wyatt a few nights later, but they found no submarine.

The next few days continued as before—filling in holes on the Malabang airstrip. Now more Jap planes were flying over Malabang than ever. One morning the cooks were filling their ten-gallon cans with water for making chow when the roar of aircraft made them look up. Almost immediately they saw our patch of sky filled by a Jap plane, flying so low the cooks could see under each wing the red ball, symbol of the Japanese Empire, and even the pilot's face—he looked directly at the three cooks and 1st Sgt. John Chandler, who happened to be talking with them. The four just froze and stared back. The Jap had just flown off when we heard an explosion and gunfire, apparently at our airstrip.

Thinking the Jap would be back, the cooks and Chandler got under the largest tree around the spring as the firing at the airstrip continued. Then the plane did come back. The fighting 14th Squadron jumped into their foxholes—not caring that they were filled with water on this low ground. The pilot now glimpsed the cooks and Chandler near the big tree and banked to get a clear shot at them. But they slipped around to the other side. Whenever the Jap circled to get a clear shot, the cooks and Chandler ducked to the other side of the trunk. After the Jap had given up and flown away, Chandler exclaimed, "Isn't this a hell of a note— playing 'hide and seek' with a Jap pilot."* Chandler, a tall blond from

*Mapes, The Butchers, the Baker, page 56.

Mississippi, was the top noncom of the 14th Squadron. Like myself, the expansion at Hickam Field had brought him rapid promotions. But he had started as a corporal, while I had started as a private.

After the Jap had left, our men at the airstrip hurried into camp and reported they also had been caught unaware. Some dived into dugouts and manned the machine guns that Captain Wyatt had set up there, ready to fire. One man had run to the tractor and fired its mounted machine gun. The pilot, surprised at drawing fire, climbed out of range just in time. But all of us had the sickening feeling that the pilot would return with companions for a real attack now that our hideout had been found out.

I was feeling pretty good until one morning I became nauseous and had chills, so I went to sick call. The corpsman found my temperature to be just slightly above normal and told me to take it easy for a day or two. But the next day my temperature had risen to 105.6°. Now the corpsman informed Dr. Heidger. The Major immediately hustled me into a staff car and drove me 15 miles north past Lake Lanao and onward to the Philippine hospital at Momungan. He left me there too weak to worry about being in the hands of the Filipinos and away from my outfit. But after intravenous injections and a few days of complete rest, I bounced back and felt very fit. During my short stay, the attractive Filipino nurses washed, ironed, and repaired all my clothing and refused any payment. It was a pleasant vacation in a relatively high and cool area—I regretted reporting back to duty. Yet there was a war going on and we were shorthanded at the airfield. So why should I loaf in a hospital where these cute nurses might give me ideas.

I returned to my outfit on January 27. In talking to the boys I found that after delivering me to the hospital, Major Heidger had come back to camp and really chewed out the corpsman who had not recognized the symptoms of malaria on my first sick call visit. While I was gone, our camp had moved a few miles on January 21 to higher ground. I was appointed Sergeant of the Guard for our new location. We had four machine gun positions—two guarding the road parallel to our bivouac and two on our end of the airfield. These positions, plus two sentries with Springfield rifles at either end of the camp, made up our guard. Although the guard was not strong, it was efficient for what it was meant to do—to keep the camp from being surprised by wandering Moros and keep watch for ship movements in the Moro Gulf.

I was on duty from 6 P.M. to 6 A.M. every night and would check my guards' posts every hour. At midnight I made coffee and sandwiches and took them to the guards. That Moro coffee was really rough—after a couple of cups, none of us could have slept if we wanted to.

The voices of the jungle were terrifying until one became used to them. I was still jumpy one night as I headed back to camp to make the usual snack for the men on guard. I was almost there when a sudden movement and rustling in the bushes startled me. I pulled my automatic .45 pistol out of its holster. But just as the pistol cleared the holster, it fired into the ground. The noise aroused the whole camp. The excited men crowded around me, but we could not find what had spooked me—probably some jungle creature.

The excitement turned to ribbing. Someone said, "What are you trying to do, sergeant? Keep us alert in case some Moros wander into camp." I was really embarrassed—especially when it took the men half an hour to settle down and hit the sack.

The next morning, before sleeping in, I dismantled the automatic pistol and found a rusty prong that probably had caused it to fire by itself. The mechanism of this pistol, which was issued to each of us, was so complicated that it was not popular. In the afternoon I walked over to the nearby Philippine Army camp and traded for the simpler .45 revolver, which was issued to the Filipinos.

One night, as I entered the sleeping camp, I heard a shuffling and turned my flashlight on a large monkey carrying a stalk of bananas over his shoulders. I drew my pistol, but it was too late. He had scrambled into the jungle. Before turning in, I thought I'd like a banana. But the stalk I'd hung on my bunk was gone—I suddenly realized it was *my* bananas that the monkey had taken.

Monkeys were very common; in fact, our squadron mascot was a small nondescript monkey named Bertha, who delighted in sitting on 1st Sgt. John L Chandler's bunk. When Chandler came to lie down, Bertha would sometimes jump up and down while chattering and spitting at him in rage. Then the 1st Sgt. would chase Bertha through the camp until she climbed a tree, stopped on a lower limb, and there scream and swear in the vilest language a monkey could manage. She was usually not nasty-tempered, however. The men would cuddle her in their arms like a baby, and she would dig in their beards or hair and purr in delight like a kitten. She was the closest facsimile to a woman any of us knew in those days, and was fed and treated with only the best of food and care.

Life became rather monotonous in the jungle, and everything was peaceful, although we knew that all hell could break loose at any time. Our main contact with the outside world was a powerful sending and receiving radio which Sgt. Beck and Cpl. William Knortz operated. Beck had suffered memory loss from a bomb which missed the *Mayon* but dropped near him while he swam for shore. But now Beck could handle our radio station effectively.

Our squadron and Filipino soldiers stationed close by gathered every day to listen to the "Voice of Freedom" broadcast from Corregidor. It gave exaggerated accounts of American successes there. The Filipinos hung on every encouraging word, and believed the promises of bombers and supplies from the south—presumably from Australia. The American soldiers knew better; but our morale and determination to survive did not waver, even though we could not imagine how we were to escape our present fix—far from the comforts and security of home.

Our motor pool crew improvised pulleys for lifting vehicles for overhaul. They salvaged parts from wrecked vehicles and even aircraft. Officers from the 81st Infantry Division came to have their staff cars and trucks repaired. The motor pool also helped the radiomen build a radio from salvaged equipment—Knortz and Beck used it to send and receive coded messages, but they would not tell anything about the messages, even to curious officers.

IV

PBY Flying Boats

April 20, 1942, to May 1, 1942

Our peaceful existence near Malabang did not last long. On April 20 we broke camp and moved back to Camp Keithley. But we only stayed overnight before turning around and moving back south along the west shore of Lake Lanao to Bacolod Grande—a good-sized Moro village. It was midway between Camp Keithley at the north end of the lake and Genassi at the south end.

It was a very attractive village with an elaborate building for Islam worship and many houses bordering the lake. Most dwellings along the shore had canoes that were tied to the stilts on which the houses were built. Few white men had dared enter before we came, because the Moros had little love of Christians—regardless of race or color. Until then we had just traded with the Moros, but now we were to camp in their midst.

Our campsite stood in the middle of the property of an important Moro chief, who was mayor of the village. Our CO, Lt. Draper, emphasized the importance of getting along with the Moros, since we were all soon to be fighting Japs. The mayor would furnish men to guard our camp and equipment. However, being close to the village, and in the chief's valuable coffee grove, brought problems.

The first difficulty arose when the cooks drove our mess truck off the main road toward the kitchen site. Angry shouts stopped the driver, but only after he ran over several ancient graves. We had driven through a graveyard where generations of the important families of Bacolod Grande were buried. We apologized, but now and then a forgetful Yank would tread on a grave and cause more turmoil. Or a soldier would accidentally damage or destroy a coffee tree. The owner-chief would immediately appear and had to be appeased with an elaborate apology. It happened more than once and caused great embarrassment.

After dark, nearly half the male population of the village carried out the chief's promise to guard the camp. They would stand all night and most of the day a short distance from our kitchen and camp—just staring at us with their mouths open. Neither rain, sun, insects, hunger, thirst, or fatigue bothered them as long as they could watch. They crowded into the kitchen and got in the cooks' way. When they tampered with kitchen equipment, the cooks pushed them back. But the Moros were resentful and backed away very slowly, with awful scowls on their faces. The next day they would push closer again.

We didn't trust the designated guards furnished by the chief but didn't know how to tell them we didn't need them. They thought they were quite important and deserved great respect for guarding the camp. They expected more service from the kitchen than our own soldiers, demanding coffee at any hour of the day or night. Nevertheless, they fell asleep while on guard duty, and the cooks missed items from the kitchen.

Other Moros would squat on their haunches for hours with home-made rifles and sharp daggers, called krises, in their laps while silently watching every move we made. Yet they had friendly looks on their faces. They wore colorful clothes, while the intricate braid on their fezzes showed their rank in Moro society. Apparently their wives—commonly each Moro had more than one—did the farming and other work of the household.

At night it was practically impossible to be alert enough to spot a Moro before he was in front of you, smilingly saying, "Hello, Joe!" Thank God they were on our side. Although they were of little help, at least they did not hinder our operations to any great extent.

The Moros let us sleep wherever there was space in the village. It was no longer crowded because many women and children had been evacuated to the mountainous interior. A large frame building with a tin roof was soon filled with GIs, who had been getting wet daily because we were in the rainy season. Kukie, the squadron drunk, and his drinking buddy burst in one evening after too much tuba and gin and woke us all up. The complaints that followed caused 1st Sgt. Chandler to declare, "whoever is close to those soreheads should knock hell out of them when they come in like that!" Chandler seldom showed so much aggravation—his responsibility for keeping us on good terms with the Moros must have put him on edge.

Some officers lived in Moro houses, while others lived in the command post close to the road. Two men slept in our chow truck as guards.

It was full of canned food that we had saved since our arrival on Mindanao. It was our last reserve, packed and ready to move at a moment's notice. Once some Moro kids sneaked up and pilfered a few cans before being noticed, but our guards didn't shoot—nothing would be gained by raising the ire of the villagers.

At Bacolod Grande I made the acquaintance of Mohammed Ali, a Moro datu, or chief. He showed me his collection of ceremonial daggers. They were six to eight inches, long with a curved marble handle and a wide, double-edged blade that tapered from the hilt to the point of the dagger. On each side of the blade was a slot to let the blood flow from the victim as the blade was withdrawn. I admired the daggers so much that Ali gave me three of them of varying sizes to start my collection.

Ali honored me by introducing me to his elderly father, who had the higher rank of sultan. The father was suspicious of me until Ali explained that I was a friend and was here to defend his people from the hated Japs. Then the Sultan softened quite a bit and showed me a photograph of some of the U.S. soldiers who finally defeated the Filipinos—they had resisted the U.S. occupation of the Philippines after the U.S. took the country from Spain in 1898. In this picture the Sultan pointed out his father, also a sultan, standing beside an American officer. Underneath the American was the signature, "Lt. J. Pershing, U.S. Army."* Ali swore the signature was genuine, and I believed him, since a Moro will not tell a lie—which is forbidden by the *Koran*, his holy scriptures.

One of Ali's men showed me a handmade rifle that was astounding. It had a crude wooden stock on which a shotgun barrel was loosely fitted. The barrel was secured by two metal rings that let the barrel move forward and backward. There was no trigger mechanism for firing. Instead, the barrel was jammed back against a fixed firing pin—a nail. I watched the man fire it—fire and smoke erupted with a roar, but, amazingly, he was not hurt. The Moro offered to let me fire it, but I declined as gracefully as I could.

At Bacolod Grande I learned of a fanatical religious ceremony by which Moro soldiers would prepare for life-or-death combat. It was called "going juramentado." The soldiers would begin by drinking copious quantities of tuba, made from fermented coconut—a horrible-tasting and potent drink. Next they would bind their genitals up in a way that caused great pain and drink some more tuba. By then they would be in such pain that they were numb to any injury that an enemy might inflict on them. In the Spanish-American War the charging Moros could not be stopped

---

*Pershing, later the famous general in World War I, apparently had fought in Bacolod Grande—we were shown trenches at the supposed battle site.

by the .38 caliber pistol used by the Americans. I was told that the larger bore .45 revolver and .45 automatic weapon were developed primarily to stop the charging Moro soldiers.

The purpose of our moving to Bacolod Grande was to prepare camouflage for two U.S. Navy PBY flying boats and be ready to service them. They were soon to arrive from Australia, land here on the lake, and take off for Corregidor. Their mission was to evacuate nurses and Navy "brass" from the beleaguered island and take them to Australia.

Ours was a small part in this dangerous mercy mission, but we went at it with a will. We planned to hide one PBY on an island in the lake under overhanging boughs. Our relatively simple job was to cut bushy limbs from other trees and place them over the protruding wings of the PBY.

We planned to hide the other PBY in a cove along the lake—its neck was 75 yards wide and it extended 100 yards inside the main shoreline. We built 50-foot towers on both sides of the cove and stretched wire across—high above the water.

The wires formed a net on which the camouflaging material lay. With only bolos and a few saws for tools, it was an engineering feat. A few men lost their grip on the high wires while fastening leafy branches to them and fell into the water, but no one was hurt. The soaked men would clamber back up to their lofty perch. I did not get a soaking; but as I was

Navy PBY flying boat—on Lake Lanao we serviced two PBYs that flew north to evacuate nurses and Navy officers from Corregidor. (National Air and Space Museum, SI Neg. No. A-42511)

cutting palm tree fronds, my prized bolo slipped out of my hand and fell into the clear water of the cove. I could see it easily, but it was too deep to dive after and we didn't have time anyway. We were quite proud of our work. Then some colonel from General Fort's staff—Fort was the senior officer in the region—flew a plane over our handiwork and proclaimed it "no good." So we had to take it all down. Finally, all we could do in preparation was to have branches ready to cover both PBYs when they arrived.

At dawn on April 29, two PBYs settled down on Lake Lanao and maneuvered into position for us to service them. Immediately we covered them with branches as we began refueling. But we soon had a Moro problem, as recalled by Victor L. Mapes, a 14th Squadron cook. The increased boat traffic upset a Moro chief, who claimed we were encroaching on his private fishing waters. He paddled his canoe out on the lake and sat with a loaded rifle where our boats had been passing. The boys wanted to shoot him but then decided to go around his claimed piece of lake.

After dark that evening, the Navy launches towed the flying boats into deep water and churned up the placid surface so the ponderous PBYs could take off more easily. We watched them finally struggle into the air after a long run. Then they circled for altitude and headed north while all of us were praying for their safe return.

At Corregidor the enemy had celebrated the Emperor's birthday that day by attacks on the fortress island. Fires were still burning at 11 P.M. when the evacuees on shore heard the steady hum of the arriving PBYs. Forty-six Navy officers, Army nurses, and a few civilian women hurried to board, and after 30 minutes the PBYs headed south, unchallenged by enemy aircraft—the Japs usually did not fly after sunset.

Early next morning, back on Lake Lanao, we began to worry when the PBYs had not returned by daybreak. But we soon heard their steady roar. After landing, the flying boats taxied their happy passengers to where we waited with outrigger canoes to bring them ashore.

As they landed, the nurses looked tired but cheerful and passed out American cigarettes to the men. The 14th Squadron cooks had prepared enough lunch for the nurses and us, so we could all eat together. They chatted as if they were at a lawn party at home—making their company most enjoyable for us—the first American women we had seen in many months. Then they rested until mid-afternoon when the onward flights to Australia were to take off.

But there was no joy for the nurses who had arrived on the PBY that was moored by the small island—that flying boat had sprung a leak in its hull and had sunk so low in the water that the Navy pilot wouldn't even try to take off. There was no space on the other PBY—its passengers from

Corregidor already filled it to more than capacity. The only thing we could think of was to truck the scared and downcast nurses to Del Monte Air Field in hopes they could get on a final B-17 flight to Australia. But they ended up being interned by the Japanese in Manila for the duration.

The other PBY, moored in the cove, rode high in the water, and the lucky passengers quickly filled the plane. Full of fuel and loaded with people, the Navy pilot headed for open water on the 20-mile-long lake. Then the flying boat gradually picked up speed but broke water only after a run of more than two miles.

But the 14th Squadron didn't give up on the partly-sunk PBY—some of our sheet-metal men paddled out to it to see if anything could be done. After hours of repair, we pumped enough water out of the hull so the pilot was willing to try a takeoff the next day. But the plane still sat so low in the water that the pilot did not want any passengers. But some of my friends eyed the empty space and planned to sneak aboard. They asked me to join them, but I didn't believe in disobeying orders, and I doubted that this plane would be able to get in the air anyway. So four or five of my 14th Squadron friends were aboard when the Navy pilot, a commander, gunned the engines, and the plane plowed forward with streams of water pouring out of the hull. But the plane moved away without picking up speed; we saw all kinds of clothes and probably tools being thrown out of the plane in hopes it would be able to lift off. I was still thinking I was glad not to be on it when it finally broke from the water five miles away and began an ascent so slow we worried it would not clear the tall trees on shore.

At a 14th Squadron reunion years later, I noticed an Air Force captain who looked familiar, but I couldn't believe he was one of the stowaways. Yet he was, and he told me that during the flight to Australia, the pilot had discovered the Air Corps boys and was furious. After he landed in Australia, he turned the culprits over to the Air Corps authorities. The Air Corps captain who took custody of the stowaways promised to convene a court-martial to handle these deserters. Satisfied that justice would be done, the Navy pilot departed. But he did not know that he had turned over the prisoners to an officer of the 14th Squadron. Instead of court-martial, the captain, a pilot, assigned the boys to appropriate enlisted slots in the Air Corps. As a pilot he may have felt a little guilty that he and the other Air Corps pilots had all been evacuated from the Philippines while the enlisted men had been left behind. Yet it was an intelligent decision because the Air Corps needed all the help it could find to stem the frightening Japanese advances in the early part of the Pacific war.

V

Under General Fort

May 1, 1942, to May 27, 1942

While we were servicing the PBYs, the Japanese landed at Parang on the Moro Gulf, 40 miles to the south, and began advancing toward us. Philippine troops and Moros, organized into a Bolo Battalion, passed by our camp in trucks, heading southward to face the invading Japanese. They were all under General Fort's command, which included all ground troops in the region.

To our consternation, we would soon be following those ground troops southward to halt the Japanese if possible. This was because the 14th Squadron had been transferred to General Fort's command. The men were not happy. We had had no infantry training, which develops fighting skills, teamwork, and the frame of mind for ground combat.

Of course, this change seemed logical to the Air Corps high command. Since no more planes were being flown on Mindanao for us to service, why not give us to General Fort to help him fight the veteran Japanese troops? Our maintenance skills in the Air Corps had not been valuable enough to justify space on the last transport flights to Australia.

These flights, however, did carry all of the Air Corps officers who were pilots—they were badly needed for future air operations. Different pilots had served as our CO until we moved our camp to higher ground while we maintained the Malabang airstrip. But at that time, 2nd Lt. Draper, who was not a pilot, became our CO. He had joined the 14th Squadron after the war started. Like us, he had had no chance of being evacuated to Australia.

On May 2, General Fort's first order to Lt. Draper was to move the

14th Squadron south to join in the defense of Genassi at the south end of Lake Lanao. But the inexperienced lieutenant led the 14th Squadron north along the Lake, away from the enemy. We hadn't gotten far when a staff car screeched to a halt in front of our column. A furious major got out of the car. It was Major Forte, a new member of General Fort's staff. On the spot, Forte put Lt. Draper under arrest and appointed our first sergeant, John Chandler, as acting CO of the Squadron. Then he ordered Chandler to turn the squadron around and head toward the enemy forces. But our stop for the night was Bacolod Grande again.

At our old camp, Chandler told us to be ready to move again soon. He said we should turn in for the night and get a good rest because this might be the last good rest we would have in a long time. But we could not sleep. We began talking in low tones. Many promises were made that whoever survived would visit the families of their fallen comrades. Gradually talk died down, but not many went to sleep. Each was thinking of what tomorrow might bring. Our outfit had been on the run for five months; we were now supposed to fight a battle we had little chance of winning. Some thought they might have a better chance of surviving by heading for the hills and eventually engaging in guerrilla warfare.

John Chandler, our new CO, knew of these thoughts, and the next morning challenged us either to get ready to fight or grab our packs and take off. In a way, many of the men wanted to go, but none did. Then Chandler deployed us just south of Bacolod Grande in a line that extended from the lakeside road far back in the jungle toward the nearby mountains. As our men were looking for good machine gun locations, Moro landowners threatened them with weapons. We had to buy them off with large amounts of emergency money—they did not know that it had little permanent value. We were disliking the Moros more and more but had strict orders to avoid any confrontation—to keep them on our side in the fight against the Japanese.

Those near the road dug in and stood by with Molotov cocktails, which Captain Wyatt had passed out. They had been made with beer bottles, gasoline, pine tar, and wicks. Captain Wyatt took Knortz and a few others ahead to be ready to mine the road and construct tank traps in front of the enemy.

We stayed in our positions hour after hour, chilled by the damp air blowing in from the lake and under constant attack by mosquitoes. The continuous lapping of waves and sounds of birds and frogs bored us. Yet we were startled by the sudden rustling of the wind in the tree tops or underbrush, the scurry of a frightened animal, or falling limbs. Chandler sent two privates back to camp on an errand, but that was the last we saw of them. Later we found one of our half-ton trucks along the road going north. Then the two had taken to the hills, where one died of malaria and the other was never found.

When Major Schroeder, a civilian planter near Malabang, came with orders from General Fort, Chandler had us assemble from our deployment. Schroeder told us we were to move south as far as we could before daylight to stall the Japs before they reached Bacolod Grande. After the retreat from Lake Dupow, General Fort was going to make another stand at Genassi, a crucial Japanese objective. There the highway divided: one fork led northward along the west side of Lake Lanao past Bacolod Grande to Dansalan, and the other turned eastward along the south side of the lake.

It was still dark when we climbed on our trucks and headed toward Genassi. Nobody cracked jokes because everybody expected the worst when we came up against the enemy's well-armed veteran foot soldiers. Some of our men had only .45 caliber automatic pistols with little ammunition, while others carried outdated Enfield rifles that were dangerous to fire because they might explode in the user's face. Our new CO, Chandler, had only a shotgun. Worse, we had no planes to attack the enemy and protect us from strafing and bombing. We also lacked tanks to deal with theirs.

As day was breaking on May 2, 1942, we reached the southern end of Lake Lanao and entered the Moro village of Genassi. The enemy was expected to reach the village from the south by a road that led through a pass just above us. I immediately feared that our position was dangerous—the village was a trap because it was like the bottom of a bowl and was surrounded on three sides by high ground or mountains. That morning General Fort's 81st Philippine Division, the Air Corps soldiers, and the Moro Bolo Battalion had all crowded into the village.

Major Robert H. Vesey of the 81st Philippine Division was in charge of the Allied forces and was still deploying his men when a Japanese tank appeared in the pass above the village. It began to fire down at us. In minutes some Filipino troops had vanished into the hills on either side, and others joined Americans on crowded trucks that jammed the escape road going north along the west shore of the lake.

I know I wasn't the first to get out of there, but I wasn't the last either. I wasn't a hero, but a .30 caliber, 1903 rifle isn't much protection against a tank. I caught a ride with 1st Sgt. Chandler, who was now acting squadron CO, and Cpl. Knortz. When we reached Bacolod Grande, we loaded our ammunition stored there on a truck. Then Knortz and I drove it around the north end of the lake and delivered the ammo to General Fort's headquarters at Bubong.

We were on our way back to Bacolod Grande when Captain Charles Wyatt, an engineering officer on General Fort's staff, ordered us to guard his personal belongings in the Dansalan Hotel instead of continuing on to Bacolod Grande. It was an enjoyable detail since the hotel doubled as the Officers' Club. It was now deserted, but dinner was on the table and champagne in the cupboard, so we feasted and had plenty to drink. After a hot shower, we took Captain Wyatt's belongings to a hotel room with us and went to bed under nice, clean sheets. Before we fell asleep, however, we heard a racket down in the kitchen. We grabbed our guns and rushed downstairs. It was not exactly the enemy, though. We got there in time to see a frightened Moro running out the door with some food and drink. We did not bother to shoot.

The next morning we filled our canteens with champagne, took a few bottles with us, and climbed on our truck. We didn't see the sense of guarding Captain Wyatt's belongings any longer, so we headed south for Bacolod Grande, where we had left our CO, Sgt. Chandler, the day before.

The Dansalan Hotel became the American officers' club and then Japanese headquarters for holding POWs at Camp Keithley. (National Archives SC-316472)

There Knortz and I helped load the squadron equipment to move it away from the enemy. But we noticed that many of the 14th Squadron were no longer with us. In the confused retreat of the last two days they had faded into the hills rather than risk capture by the advancing enemy forces. We had been ordered not to desert and threatened with court-martial if we did. I stayed, although I thought a lot about getting away.

Large numbers of Filipinos were also still "going over the hill," and Captain Jay Navin, CO of the Philippine 81st Regiment, asked me and other 14th Squadron noncoms to accept commissions as third lieutenants in his regiment—we would command platoons, halt desertions, and boost the morale of his troops. But I was not interested, and I do not believe any American NCO took up the offer.

During the next night the 14th Squadron men still on hand were ordered to move northward along Lake Lanao and around its north end to General Fort's headquarters at Bubong. There we gathered our supplies and equipment. But then we had to move everything again six or seven miles up the mountainside to a hospital site General Fort had chosen. The trail was too steep for even a motorcycle, so we had to move everything by foot—it took from about May 5 to May 15 to complete the job. It would have taken much longer if a lot of loyal Filipinos and Moros had not helped us. We finally set up "Camp Palao" high up the mountain, surrounded by very thick jungle.

In the meantime, on May 6 General Wainwright had surrendered the Philippine and American forces on Bataan and Corregidor. Now there were no large forces in the Philippines to face the enemy head-on. We waited at Camp Palao, believing that General Fort would carry on guerrilla warfare in the hills with the American, Philippine, and Moro soldiers he still controlled—Fort was a veteran of 43 years, mostly served in the Philippines, and was loved and respected by both Filipinos and Moros.

But General Fort's dream of guerrilla warfare "blew away" when General Sharpe ordered him to surrender all his soldiers rather than continue the fight. Sharpe explained that General Homma threatened to execute the prisoners taken on Bataan and Corregidor unless surrenders were accomplished throughout the Philippines.

When the Moros found out that we were about to surrender, they became eager to secure any of our weapons that struck their fancy, figuring we would have no use for them. One Moro wanted to buy the 7.65 mm German Luger pistol I had bought at a pawn shop in Honolulu. I had already used the 100 rounds of ammunition that came with the gun— most of them expended without result in firing at monkeys in the tree-tops while I was at Bacolod Grande. But the lack of ammunition did not bother the Moro. He assured me, "That's okay, Joe, I can make the 'bollots'." I learned later that the Moros had forges in the hills, where they could produce knives, swords, and the wavy-edged kris, as well as molds for "bollots" and cartridges for different-sized weapons. But I didn't sell my Luger. Instead, I sealed it in a metal can and buried it.

At this time there was an aftermath to the battlefield replacement of Lt. Draper as 14th Squadron Commander by 1st Sgt. Chandler—Major Forte had put Draper under arrest shortly before the clash at Genassi. But then Major Luther Heidger, 19th Bomb Group Flight Surgeon, had temporarily taken command of the 14th squadron until the paperwork for Chandler's promotion could be completed. Now Heidger called in Sgt. Chandler and me to inform us that he had made out an order for the promotion of 1st Sgt. Chandler to second lieutenant, and for my promotion to squadron first sergeant. As the replacement for Chandler, I would then be the ranking noncom in the squadron. But General Fort believed that the promotions would be pointless since he had decided to follow General Sharpe's orders to surrender. Fort's refusal to make me first sergeant probably saved my life.

By the day of surrender, May 26, there were only 46 Americans and about 300 Filipinos in General Fort's command—all that was left of the 14th Squadron and the Philippine 81st Division, plus a few other Air Corps men. We straggled out of the jungle and gathered at Bubong to hear the General's final instructions. He walked firmly out of his headquarters' shack—an erect, gray-haired figure. I felt sorry for him because of this depressing end to a long Army career. As the General spoke, two Japanese officers stood impassively in the background. Strangely, I felt no hate or repulsion when I looked at them. They wore strange-looking uniforms and had slant eyes, but otherwise looked like Filipinos. Suddenly I concluded they were Japanese who may have lived in the Philippines as long-term spies—thus they would know English and were there to report to the enemy command what General Fort was saying to us. They said nothing, and we ignored them.

General Fort sadly explained why he had to surrender—General Homma threatened to execute the American prisoners he had taken on Bataan and Corregidor unless all American and Philippine forces in the Philippines were surrendered. After he spoke, one of his officers told us to shave off our beards, cut each other's hair, and put on clean uniforms—that last order was not possible, but we tried to comply with the rest. The officer said we should put on a good appearance since we were U.S. soldiers.

Then the General broke in and said he had something for us if we would line up in front of a table where an officer sat with a pile of

Philippine money. General Fort's Moro aide had cleaned out the Dansalan Bank and Printing Office during the retreat through Dansalan to Bubong. Now, Fort's last gesture was to distribute the money to us—500 pesos to each officer and 300 to each soldier. It was a nice gesture, but we did not see how it could be of any use.

VI

Surrender and Death March

May 26, 1942, to July 18, 1942

Shortly after dawn on May 27, our small group of Americans and General Fort's 300 Filipinos plodded away from Bubong—the beginning of a six-mile hike to Japanese headquarters at Dansalan. We carried our side arms empty and our rifles over the shoulder, with stock to the rear and bolt open. It was a silent column of bedraggled men—even normally talkative soldiers had nothing to say. Our faces showed our hate for our situation.

The Japanese staff met us in a large park in the center of Dansalan, where we threw our rifles in one pile and our side arms in another. The Japanese commander gave us a speech in broken English—he said something about our not being prisoners but, rather, "guests of the emperor."

Later we were quartered in an abandoned building, which had been the mint for producing provincial money—some of which was in our pockets, thanks to General Fort. Life was not too bad. We had our own mess, prepared by Jimmy Palmer and Vic Mapes, who used pesos to buy rice, meat, and vegetables from the stores in town. The Japanese liked not having to worry about feeding us.

There were some women interned in a building next to ours. When Japanese soldiers started to molest them with crude advances, the Japanese commander gave us clubs to guard the women's house against any of his amorous soldiers. I was on this detail a few times and certainly felt foolish doing guard duty with a club that I was to use against Japanese soldiers armed with rifles and bayonets. However, no Japanese bothered us or the women once the guard was established.

While we were prisoners at the printing press, Jap soldiers would make nightly visits to American officers who were quartered on the top floor. They brought sake and wanted to party with our officers, who could not say no. They joined the Japs in drinking toasts and singing songs—the Japs' favorite was "Auld Lang Syne." This was amusing at first but got old fast, especially when the raucous singing continued into the night while we were trying to sleep below. More galling, we had to stand at attention while the visiting Japs paraded through the building with rifles and fixed bayonets, and clanked up the stairs with hob-nailed boots. Sometimes they would come late at night, drunk, and awaken us. We were quick to obey their order to stand at attention, fearing one of them might stick a bayonet into a laggard.

Nevertheless, worse was yet to come. These rough-and-ready soldiers moved on, probably to more combat duty. Their replacements were occupation troops—extremely young men and a number of veterans too old to keep up with the front-line fighting. We soon learned the difference.

At muster the new Japs foisted a new counting system on us. The previous Japs had counted us twice daily, but the replacements forced us to count ourselves by calling out Japanese numbers in sequence as we stood in formation. Anyone slow in learning Japanese numbers or made a mistake received a hard slap on each cheek. It was better to line up in the middle of the formation because prisoners in the front rank or ends of ranks were convenient targets, and often were slapped when anyone missed the count.

About June 10, 1942, the guards invaded our quarters with fixed bayonets and searched each of us for any item of Japanese origin. They seemed to be looking for things taken from Japanese civilians who were imprisoned by Filipino authorities after the war started. The soldiers also wanted the contents of Japanese stores that had been confiscated. During the search, the Japs abused and beat us severely, giving rise to urgent talk of escape. We were disgusted with the American officers who had talked us into surrender on the grounds that the Japs would treat us well—a far cry from what was happening. The next night the Japs stormed in and woke us up in the middle of the night. The roll call showed everyone to be there—our escape talk had only been talk. But the Japs and our officers, who were standing by, were surprised that no one had vanished. (It looked like our own officers had betrayed us to stop an escape.) The Japs were jumpy and picked out some of us at random to beat up. After they left, Major Heidger gave us another lecture and repeated his threat to bring desertion charges against any who escaped.

While being held at the mint building in Dansalan, we heard rumors that Moros had killed several Jap soldiers, who had probably been ambushed on the Dansalan-Genassi road along the west shore of Lake Lanao. The Japs patrolled this road regularly, but the Moros living there thought this region belonged to them. Hoping to quiet down the Moros, the Japanese did a lot of practice firing of guns and elaborate bayonet drills in public—but to no avail. Two Moros with long, wavy-edged krises continued to hang around the mint building every day, looking like they were ready to kill more Japs. Finally, on June 14, the nervous Japs moved us across the Agus River into Camp Keithley. Here the guards were less jittery because it was easier to keep the Moros at a distance. For our part, instead of the floor, we now slept on metal beds in the barracks that still stood—the retreating Filipinos had burned some of the buildings to keep them from being used by the enemy.

After our move, the Japanese soldiers' chase after women seemed more successful. When held at the mint, we had been given clubs to protect interned women from being molested by Japanese soldiers. But now so many Japs were contracting venereal disease from the local population that they kept Major Heidger, our doctor, busy treating them, according to Vic Mapes. We were amused by the Dansalan women's success in weakening the enemy garrison.

Treatment improved after our move to Camp Keithley on June 14. But we were put on an "honor system" not to attempt an escape. They told us that our commanding officer, company commander, and first sergeant would be executed in the event of escape. We considered this fair enough, but I was thankful I had not been promoted to first sergeant. Furthermore, we could go into town if we had a pass that was signed by Colonel Eugene Mitchell, who had been appointed the commanding officer of the American prisoners by the Japanese commander. The Colonel was a good man at dealing with the Japanese, who respected him very much.

The Japanese formed us into work parties to repair buildings in Dansalan that the Moros had burned and looted after we retreated toward Bubong. We worked mostly without a guard. After our morning and evening roll calls, Colonel Mitchell reported our status to the Japanese commander at his headquarters in the Dansalan Hotel.

Our experience at night was worse than in the daytime. Any of us could be awakened in the dark by a leering Japanese guard who would then motion with his shining bayonet for some item in the American's pack. There was nothing to do but give it to him. After Col. Mitchell reported this nuisance to the camp commander, it stopped to some degree but not entirely.

At Camp Keithley the Japs assigned General Fort to a private room, and he kept to himself much of the time. Yet, our erect, composed commanding officer, who looked like a general, would wander into the kitchen and praise the cooks, and talk with enlisted prisoners and his officers at other times. The general made his own cigars out of strong native tobacco sold by the Moros. He would place a cigar upright in his pipe and smoke it.

One evening I came upon him smoking on the barracks porch and staring across Lake Lanao toward his hideout in the mountains where he had expected to continue the fight against the Japanese. His cigar had almost turned into ashes when I greeted him. He wanted to chat and told me that he had been a young American soldier in the Philippines during the Spanish-American War, and then had settled near Lake Lanao. Since then he had risen to command of the Philippine Constabulary forces in the region. But now he was ending his military career as a prisoner and could not wage the guerrilla warfare that he had planned. He looked at me and said, "What a way to finish my career of 43 years in the Army." I had no appropriate reply, but I mumbled something and he knew I understood how desolate he felt.

Another evening I was coming back from the latrine after dark when I heard quiet voices outside General Fort's quarters. Keeping in the shadows, I got closer and saw that the General was talking to a Moro civilian. As I listened I realized the Moro was actually Lt. Ali, who had befriended me in Bacolod Grande before our surrender.

Now Ali had somehow slipped past the Jap guard to talk with General Fort. The lieutenant informed the general that he had a battalion of well-trained Moros in the hills, just waiting for the general's orders to retake Camp Keithley so the Americans could take to the hills and join in guerrilla warfare against the Japanese. Fort replied that he was a soldier and his orders had been to surrender. Otherwise he would endanger the lives of the thousands of prisoners who had been taken on Bataan—General Homma had threatened to execute the Bataan prisoners if other troops in the Philippines did not surrender.

Lt. Ali nodded and said he understood. Then he said that later that night he would bring in an American by the name of Childress who had been booed by a Moro while he slept. That night Ali brought the wounded man in—again past the Japanese guard, who was drunk. I had never seen a drunken Jap guard on duty, but he surely was—probably the work of Ali.

The next day Childress told me that he owned a coconut plantation on Mindanao. But when the Japs landed at Parang, Childress had volunteered for duty. Then after the tank fired into Genassi, Childress was separated from his unit and wandered in the jungle for days—he was not familiar with the Lake Lanao region. Finally, after falling asleep on the side of a trail, a Moro attacked him, took his rifle, and left him unconscious— deeply slashed on the left side by the Moro's bolo. A member of Lt. Ali's staff found Childress and brought him in. Lacking medical supplies, Lt. Ali had brought Childress to our POW camp in the belief that our Major Heidger would be able to take care of him. In the days that followed, Childress improved under Major Heidger's care.

Four men in our camp had planned to escape before they became prisoners—Cpl. William Knortz, Pvt. Robert Ball, and Seamen Jas. S. Smith and William Johnson of the PT boats. Before the surrender, they had sealed arms, ammunition, and quinine in an ammunition box and buried it near Bubong. Now all four of them worked together on a night detail, caring for water pumps on the lake shore. They were trusted and came and went as they pleased.

Cpl. Knortz was the leader of the four and approached me quite often and told me they had everything arranged to escape. But they said "Tonight's the night" so often we came to take it as a joke. Major Heidger learned of the escape talk and told us the Japanese were not kidding about the executions that would follow an escape attempt. When Knortz invited me to escape with them, I was tempted, but then decided I didn't want the death of a colonel, captain, and 1st sergeant on my conscience. Anyhow, the chances of escape were slim, and there was more danger from the Moros after our surrender. Some of them resented the Americans surrendering and turning over our gear and supplies to the Japanese—they had jeered us along the road when we marched down the road to turn over our arms to the enemy.

Vic Mapes, assigned to keep on cooking for us, remembers an upsetting incident in late July. One evening a commotion between our barracks and the Filipinos' buildings caused us to rush outside. First we saw several Japanese soldiers standing around a struggling horse. It was a fine riding horse that Mapes had trained and ridden at Camp Keithley before the surrender. Now the Japs were stabbing the beast again and again with their bayonets. This cruelty revolted us, but we knew it was dangerous to show how we felt. We learned later that this torture came about because the spirited horse had thrown a Japanese officer, who had abused him.

But that wasn't the whole story. Now Mapes had to grind up burgers from his pet horse. The Japs stood watching to see us eat the horse. Some of us slipped their burgers to those who were able to eat them. Bill Knortz, who was always talking about making a break, declared, "If the Japs can torture a dumb animal, just think what would happen to us if we are stupid enough to stick around. I'm fed up, and I'm going to get out of this mess, no matter what!"

On July 1, 1942, Knortz and his three most likely companions, Johnson, Ball, and Smith, failed to report back to the barracks at 6 A.M. after their night shift. After waiting two hours, Col. Mitchell reported the absent men to the Japanese commander. Japanese guards immediately surrounded the barracks and kept us inside except to go to the latrine. The guards came inside and began to loot in earnest. A guard grabbed my complete Philippine Army pack and gave me an empty Dutch pack in exchange. That night the guards stomped in and out of the barracks all night—while we wondered what they would do in retaliation for the escape.

The next morning, four men who slept near the escapees were taken across the river to Japanese headquarters at the Dansalan Hotel. They were Peterson, Settrini, Kuhn, and Hughes. They had no idea where the escapees had gone and knew nothing about their escape, but the Japanese soldiers threw them around jiu-jitsu style and bellowed at them. They finally returned to the barracks that evening without any serious injury. But the Japanese cut our food ration and tightened restrictions on us.

On July 3, a Japanese interpreter came to the barracks and took away Col. Vesey, Captain Price, and 1st Sgt. Chandler to headquarters for questioning. Later we saw the three of them walking around in circles near the Japanese headquarters, which was across the river about 500 yards distant. After an hour or so, they were taken somewhere out of sight. We never saw them again, but that evening the interpreter who had taken them away reported that "they had died like soldiers." Nobody asked how they were killed, but we figured they served as bayonet practice dummies.

Thus the Japanese mainly carried out their threat to execute our commanding officer, company commander, and 1st sergeant if there were even an attempt of escape. But instead of our commanding officer, General Fort, or Col. Mitchell, who was next in rank, the Japanese had taken Col. Vesey. It was unclear why General Fort was spared. However, Col. Mitchell may have been spared because they liked him and he had reported the escape. The enemy chose Captain Price because he had recently taken direct charge of the enlisted prisoners, and so qualified as company commander. 1st Sgt. Chandler was the 1st sergeant, and so was the third victim of the escape—my fate if General Fort had not refused to promote me to 1st sgt.

Before the escape, we had learned that we were to be transferred to the main prison camp on Mindanao, located at Malaybalay in north central Mindanao. The camp commander had said he would furnish trucks to carry us the 25 miles to the port of Iligan—the first segment of the trip. But now the Japanese were angry over the escape and violation of their honor system. As punishment, all prisoners would walk instead of ride to Iligan.

After a looting guard had taken my Philippine Army pack, I had scrounged around and found one change of clothes, a G.I. blanket, and some toilet articles. With my pack on my back and two canteens on my belt, I fell out with the rest of the prisoners at 0800 on July 4 for the march to Iligan. They arranged the Americans four abreast into a column. Then they strung a heavy wire through the belts of the men in each of the column's four files. The lines were adjusted to marching distance, and the guards on each side of the column saw to it that the distance between the files stayed even. The Filipinos were left unwired and marched in a column ahead of us. A truckload of soldiers with a mounted machine gun followed us—waiting for someone to try to escape. On another truck, General Fort, Col. Mitchell, and Major Heidger rode with the Japanese officers.

Childress, who Major Heidger had been treating for a bad bolo slash, marched next to me on the right—I was in the extreme left file. He soon said he couldn't make it and wanted me to take his money. I refused and had him lean on my shoulder as we continued. Col. Mitchell and Major Heidger noticed us and appealed to the Japanese officers to let Childress ride in the truck. Then they stopped the column, unhooked Childress, and took him back to the truck. I thought they were being pretty decent to him until I heard the shot that ended Childress's suffering.

As the march continued, I began to think the enemy guard had done me a favor by taking my bulky Philippine Army pack and giving me this light, compact Dutch pack with thick, broad shoulder straps. It rode very comfortably on my shoulders—I was better off than the majority of the men, who carried clumsy musette bags and other uncomfortable packs loaded to the limit.

Lt. Col. Barnes of the medical corps was carrying a mattress, canned food, and a veritable library of medical books. The load caused him to slow down his whole file. The result was that Lt. Robert Pratt at the head of that file had to pull like the devil to keep his file up with the rest of the column. We tried to talk Barnes into throwing away that heavy load before he killed himself, Lt. Pratt, and the whole bunch of us—but to no avail.

At our second break—ten minutes every hour—Captain Jay Navin, who had commanded the 84th Philippine Regiment, was in bad shape from heat exhaustion and from the extra pulling burden of being in Barnes' file. He asked me for water. I handed him my canteen but insisted that he only swallow a little. Instead, he turned the canteen upside down and drank half of it before I could stop him. It was a matter of seconds before he was delirious and gasping for breath. We laid him on the ground, opened his shirt, and called Major Heidger. A watching Japanese guard motioned the Major to stay where he was and walked over and looked at the unconscious Navin. He merely grunted, pulled him off the road by his collar, and shot the captain in the forehead.

After Captain Navin was shot, Dick Beck, who was walking next to me, became very despondent and told me he was not going to make it. He had suffered from amnesia since last December when he jumped off the ship taking us to Mindanao. I told him he should lean on me and I would get him to Iligan. I was over six feet tall and still weighed about 175 pounds—our cooks, Palmer and Mapes, had continued to feed us after the surrender. Now Dick Beck, who was thin and slight in stature, threw his left arm over my shoulders, and then I carried him the best I could. He was not heavy enough to be much of a strain on me.

By 11 o'clock, the tropical, burning heat was terrible. I thanked my lucky stars that I had built myself up with all the swimming and hiking I had done in the Hawaiian Islands. After we persuaded the stubborn Lt. Col Barnes to throw away his gear, the column made better time. Even the guards couldn't keep up with us, although they walked for only one hour at a time and rested an hour while riding in the truck. They would yell at us to march faster and look on in admiration when we did go faster.

The Filipinos ahead of us had started at a lively pace—not being wired together as we were—and laughed at our slow, measured progress. But by the time we reached Iligan at six in the evening, they were in worse shape than we. Their bare feet had worn raw on the rough, rocky road, while ours were mostly protected by shoes. My only injury—outside of almost complete exhaustion—was a small blister on my left heel. I thought little of it, and it healed soon. Later, however, it became an annoying problem.

That night we were all lying cramped together on the wooden floor of a schoolhouse when we were awakened by the violent vomiting of Lt. Pratt—as the lead man of his file, Pratt had taken the brunt of pulling Lt. Col. Barnes and his heavy load on the march. He had exhausted himself to keep the column moving so as to avoid Japanese retaliation. Now Pratt could not stop his dry heaving. He tried some tomato juice offered by someone nearby, but Pratt could keep nothing in his stomach. He was delirious for some time and then he died.

We buried Lt. Pratt in the backyard of the schoolhouse where we had been sleeping. All of us and the Japanese were very tired—we were allowed to rest and sleep all day. An outdoor kitchen was set up, but all we had to eat was rationed rice and turnip greens boiled in plain water. In the afternoon the guards "shook us down" for all our money except 20 pesos, which each prisoner could keep. I had to give up 210 pesos for their sake* money.

They also helped themselves to any personal belongings that struck their fancy. We couldn't do anything about it, but, according to Vic Mapes of the 14th Squadron, ex-lieutenant, now Pvt. Draper, let out a volley of racial insults in English after a guard walked away with valuable coins Draper had gotten in trading with Moros. Unfortunately, a Jap interpreter at the other side of the room understood the insults. Yet somehow the Japs couldn't figure out who was guilty—Draper had waited a time before his blast. When the rest of the Americans wouldn't point out Draper, the Japs stomped out but promised to deal with them later—the men worried about another Death March or something else.

When the Jap guards suddenly reappeared, the men came smartly to attention. But the guards rained blows on them. They had brought Col. Mitchell, their favorite American officer, to watch the punishment. The grim Colonel informed the men that the guards were determined to shoot someone for the insulting remarks that had been made. Since no one would point out the culprit, the guards would choose someone at random to execute. But they left the prisoners alone with Col. Mitchell for five minutes to identify the real culprit before picking out someone themselves.

The men thought the inexperienced and unpopular Draper should pay for his blunder—but not by execution. But none of the men wanted to walk out and be murdered either. Col. Mitchell tried in vain to get a decision. Time was running out when the Colonel said that he would try something that might work if we stuck together.

The Japs were back after five minutes and demanded a man come forward to be shot—they pointed their guns at the Americans in case there was resistance. Now Col. Mitchell declared in a firm voice that it had been difficult to find the right man, and it would be of no use to shoot the wrong one. The men held their breath while the Japs looked displeased. But Mitchell went on, "If you do not take anyone to be shot this time, I will offer to be shot next time if the men will not point out the culprit." The Japs did not look at all satisfied, but little by little they cooled off and accepted the proposition. But they assured the Colonel that next time somebody would surely be shot.

Later that day a Japanese sergeant and guard asked for volunteers to

*Japanese alcoholic drink.

get some rice from the dock. I didn't go, but we heard what happened after the frightened men came back. The work party of eight said goodbye as though they would never see us again as they boarded a large GI truck with three guards and a driver. While passing through the ruins of Iligan, a Filipino civilian risked his life by secretly making a "V" sign for them to see—a common gesture made to American soldiers before the Japanese occupation.

Then our men reached a large dock with gaping holes and continued to where large sacks of rice lay outside a warehouse. The men were eager to load them on the truck, but the sacks were very heavy for them in their weakened condition. They loaded some sacks with great difficulty and wanted to stop, but the sergeant told them they couldn't leave until the truck was filled. The men had about reached the end of their rope when a staff car pulled to a screeching halt beside them.

An angry Jap officer with a sword in hand got out of the car. The sergeant and guard snapped to attention, saluted smartly, and yelled to the Americans at the top of their voices. The Americans dropped their bags and also stood at attention and saluted. They held their breath while the officer looked at them as if he would like to cut off their heads. Suddenly he turned to the sergeant, half-drew his sword, and tongue-lashed him for letting us out. Finally, he slapped the sergeant in the face, glared at our men, and sped away. The guards hustled the prisoners on the truck, not bothering about the sacks still on the dock. During the wild ride back, the truck came close to turning over, and our men were almost thrown out by the sudden stop at the schoolhouse. This excitement, added to the Death March and Lt. Draper's insults, had us all scared about the future.

While the rice party was gone, the Japs had demanded money for the rice being brought from the dock. To cook it, the Japs let some Filipinos out to build fires under large cauldrons. The rice took forever to steam. Finally it was ready and brought to the starving prisoners—almost 300 Filipinos on the first floor and 40 or so Americans on the second. It was easier for the Filipinos to get their share, so a few Americans took a large ammunition can out through the hungry Filipinos and filled it with rice and carried it and a small can of dried fish up to the second floor.

The next day there was no bustle to indicate the dreaded march would continue, so some slept and others mended and traded shoes. And some traded with the Filipinos downstairs. The next morning we began to stir soon after daylight. Surprisingly, we had rested fairly well, despite the cramped space.

Early the next day the Japs ordered us to get ready for the boat trip. Yet we were still afraid—we imagined being taken on the road again, with the result of quick death for the older men and those weakened by dysentery and malaria. Expecting the worst, we took as much water as possible and very little else. When the guards lined us up and marched us through town past sympathetic Filipinos, we thought the talk about a boat trip was a cruel joke.

But we kept going and reached the waterfront where a 40-foot launch, the *Tito Maru*, was tied along the dock. They ordered us all in the hold except General Fort, Col. Mitchell, and Major Heidger. We barely had standing space but were happy for the moment to be sailing instead of marching. After some bickering among the Japs, the *Tito Maru* cast off its lines and headed out to sea, leaving some Japs on the dock yelling protests. The lifting mist exposed the launch to the blazing sun, which soon made the hold unbearably hot.

Major Heidger pointed out our horrible situation to the senior Jap officer, who then decided to let one man at a time go topside to the latrine. This was relief beyond words. We organized ourselves so each trip was short enough for everyone to go more than once. From the topside reports brought back, we figured the launch was keeping the coast to its starboard side as we proceeded north. When the sun was overhead, we followed the coast eastward. During the afternoon the sun gradually sank on our stern and gave us some relief from the heat.

Yet it was still miserably hot in the hold when we docked at Cagayan—our first landing on Mindanao back on January 1. As we came up on deck at dusk, a strong wind suddenly chilled us. Our guards marched us off at a fast pace, bringing some of us to the point of collapse. We worried that the Japs wanted to get us someplace where it would be convenient to shoot stragglers. A deserted grove of coconut trees increased our foreboding, but just beyond we stopped at a yellow schoolhouse.

The guards searched each prisoner on the porch before sending him inside with orders to stay there. After we asked for food, they provided a small can of fish for each three men and a sardine can of water for each of us. But evening brought no rest. We had just finished eating when a Jap officer strode in front of us with drawn sword. He engaged in a prolonged mock combat that ended with the decapitation of his imaginary opponent. Then, after we had spread out on the floor for the night, Japs returned to make us stand at attention for a Jap major. He first wanted to speak to "Major" Fort, not realizing our senior officer was a general. The Jap wanted to be friendly with General Fort but soon gave up because of the language barrier. Then, turning to us, he claimed in broken English that he would guarantee our safety and the use of the nearby latrine, but declared we would die if disobedient or disruptive—no news to us.

After the officer left, General Fort told us he had guaranteed our good behavior in an agreement with the Jap commander whereby the Japs would take his life if we misbehaved. Now it was up to us to avoid behavior that would bring on deadly Jap reprisals. This short speech made us admire General Fort even more. Grateful for his trust, and believing we would be safer, we lay down on the floor and went to sleep.

The next morning we stirred early, some rubbing others to ease stiffness, and others exercising. But we were too hungry for much activity and soon were motionless as we hoped for chow. During this day of unusual peace and relative comfort, we read a lot. Each man found something there to suit his personality—it must have been a school library.

In the following days we learned we were to be sent to the POW camp at Malaybalay, but we didn't know whether we were to march or ride— the Japs claimed they were trying to get trucks. After nearly a week at Cagayan, the Japs told us one evening to get ready to move in the morning—July 18, 1942.

VII

Malaybalay

July 18, 1942, to September 30, 1942

On July 18, 1942, we woke up early and packed a little rice and dried minnows in our mess kits. Then, when several GI trucks drew up, driven by Filipino drivers, our anxiety about another march vanished. Riding on the truck flatbeds, we drove through the wreckage of Cagayan and past Filipinos, who gave no victory signs—either fearing Jap retaliation or no longer believing America would win. Then we headed inland as the trucks picked up speed. The rough road jolted us as we began a steep climb. When the drivers hurtled around a series of hairpin curves, we thought about being thrown down the deep ravines, even if the trucks managed not to tip over. Climbing higher, we passed grave markers for Americans, Filipinos, and Japs, as well as abandoned equipment. In the ravines beside the road lay cars and even a B-17 bomber. Then carcasses of cattle cluttered the road and still reeked at the outskirts of deserted villages.

We stopped beside some grapefruit trees outside another abandoned village. Nearby, a spring bubbled out of the ground. We drank from the spring and ate the ripe fruit with our rice and fish. By afternoon we were driving past rolling pastures and breathing the cool, fresh air at hundreds of feet above sea level. Around a turn, a grove of pines loomed, and as we got closer, one of us recognized the emergency hospital at Impalutto where he had been treated. Now there were dozens of Japanese guards about and some prisoners, who rushed toward us to see some fellow Americans.

The trucks slowed to 15 mph, and to our amazement we recognized the men running to greet us as buddies from the 14th Squadron who we thought had been killed in the fighting around Lake Lanao. We yelled our news back and forth. They told us some of the nurses there were among the evacuees from Corregidor who had been left behind at Bacolod Grande—the pilot of their PBY would not take them on to Australia. He feared his plane could not take off from the lake after the hull broke on a rock and let in too much water for the plane to handle a full load.

Our buddies at Impalutto threw pineapples to us, which we quickly hid, causing the Japs to threaten us with rifles. Although our stay was brief, our spirits remained high long after we had driven off. The Japs kept the trucks moving at a fast pace—we believed they wanted to reach a well-guarded place before dark. A steady breeze and drizzle chilled us as we jounced along.

Finally we descended into a valley and reached the edge of a good-sized town. Many Japanese and Filipinos stared sullenly at our approach. But, unseen by the Japs, two Filipinos made "V" signs as we passed. Our guards relaxed when we reached an intersection, where we stopped to await orders. The Japs searched us and said we were going to a large concentration camp. They warned us to behave—they considered us rebellious prisoners.

In a short time we reached the edge of the camp, where a guardhouse swarmed with guards. They ordered us to fall in, and in steady rain and growing darkness we marched into the large prison camp of Malaybalay. We were amazed to see many shacks with lights and the large number of prisoners—about 600 we later found out.

It had been an easy day, but those who had gorged themselves on the fresh pineapples thrown to us by our buddies at Impalutto had awful stomachaches. By next evening, however, they were able to enjoy the feast served us at the Officers' Dining Hall. We ate all we wanted of hash, carrots and peas, bread and butter with jam, cake, and coffee with milk and sugar. We sat at tables with dinnerware and were served by waiters who usually served the officers. But the waiters told us not to expect that treatment again.

General Sharpe, who surrendered all the rest of our forces in the Philippines after the fall of Corregidor, was the senior prisoner and greeted us in a friendly manner, besides arranging for the one-time dinner at the officers' mess. He had his own hut at Malaybalay. He had us make flowerbeds on each side of the path to the door of his hut. Each bed was shaped like a star, so the two of them were meant to show Sharpe's rank from the air. We thought this rather childish, but the general was a highly-respected old man, so we didn't mind planting flowers for him. He was a tall, lean man, who looked the part of a general as he walked about the camp with his swagger stick.

Malaybalay stood on a plateau at an elevation of 1800 feet, so nights were cool, although days were warm since we were near the equator. The soil was very fertile, and we were growing our own string beans, peas, corn, potatoes, squash, peanuts, and tomatoes. This produce, plus available beef, rice and gravy, bamboo sprout soup, and canned milk, should have made for a good diet.

But my Company A did not benefit because our cook, "Soup Bones" Reedy, fed us mostly rice. Furthermore, he let friends steal food. As a result, our CO relieved Soup Bones and his mess officer and replaced them with Captain Harry Katz and Staff Sgt. Jimmy Palmer—he had been a fine cook for the 14th Squadron ever since our arrival at Clark Field. In the new setup, I was the chief or "chaser" of the five-man KP crew—two of them had to constantly keep the fires going in the crude stove. Besides better main dishes, our bakers turned out buns, bread, squash turnovers, and, on Sundays, pancakes. We had plenty of white wheat flour because the Filipinos would trade their rations to us for our ration of rice flour.

Company C fed the quartermaster soldiers, so their chow was the best of all. Finally, our Captain Katz had a talk with the quartermaster officer, and Company A immediately began to receive more beef, vegetables, and pineapple juice. Things were going well until Jimmy Palmer was put in the hospital with amoebic dysentery, and I came down with acute diarrhea. Palmer's assistant, Ramirez, could not get along with the mess crew—the chow fell off again. Then the old mess sergeant, Soup Bones, and his crew came back, and their favorites began to steal again.

Meantime, the officers had become unhappy with Richard P. Hough, the manager of their mess—Jimmy Palmer had willingly transferred to our Company A mess to get away from Hough. The officers had overlooked Hough's personal use of the mess fund to buy himself candy and coca-cola. But when Hough bought these items in quantity and tried to sell them back to the officers at double his purchase price, they became incensed. Yet Hough survived in his job because Col. Chastine intervened—Chastine was overall manager of the American POWs, but subject to Japanese control.

The Philippine camp was off limits to us, but there was a market between the camps where civilian Filipinos sold local food and lots of U.S. Army canned food—probably stolen from abandoned warehouses. Americans traded clothes, shoes, or rings for food or candy. Prices were outrageously high—the peddlers must have made small fortunes. They didn't like American dollars, Philippine emergency issue, or Japanese occupation script. But they had to accept the Japanese script or be run out of camp. Their favorite was the Philippine gold peso.

The Filipino POWs could get the best bargains because they knew the sales girls and could talk the Philippine dialect. I didn't sell my high school graduation ring because I couldn't get the 10 pesos I wanted for it. The 20 pesos I brought to Malaybalay were soon gone, so I was broke. In time, the Japanese noticed the favoritism shown the Filipinos, so they posted a list of the goods that could be sold and enforced compliance. We appreciated the idea, but it didn't matter much because by that time we had little money left.

Being broke was nothing compared to the acute abdominal pains I felt after every meal. I went to sick call, which was conducted by American doctors who had the responsibility of treating us. Captain DeMoore poked my stomach here and there, gave me salt pills, and ordered an enema. When none of this helped, DeMoore told me nothing was wrong and claimed I was just "gold-bricking" to avoid the daily exercises and drill that our officers were having us do—to maintain morale and our identity as soldiers. But after each meal I still had these terrible cramps.

Finally I was too sick to go and see any doctor, so I sent my good friend, Ed Lubiewski, to fetch Major Heidger. Earlier, when the 14th was stationed at the Malabang airstrip, Dr. Heidger had driven me to a Filipino hospital because I needed immediate treatment for malaria. Now Heidger came back with Lubiewski—both dripping from the heavy rain of a raging thunderstorm. After a short examination, Heidger told me I had too much hydrochloric acid in my stomach from eating too much rice. He gave me some pills that ended my pain almost at once.

A doctor who was supposed to treat us was Lt. Col. Barnes—he had slowed up our Death March to Iligan by trying to carry too much personal gear, thus burdening a fellow marcher, Lt. Pratt, and contributing to his collapse and death that night. Barnes drank too much and was too old to be an effective doctor. Captain DeMoore and another young doctor did not have our confidence, so we depended on Major Heidger.

At Malaybalay we actually held a prisoner inside the American section of the camp. The Japanese had caught an American, named Rice, walking boldly out of the camp. The guards brought him to Col. Chastine. They said that Rice must be crazy to do a thing like that, so they wanted to shoot him. But Chastine thought it would be better to keep as much control of discipline as possible in American hands. Therefore Chastine obtained permission from the Japanese command to build a stockade in the American section to confine Rice. However, we figured there was "method to Rice's madness." He had griped loudest about Company A's chow. But in the stockade Rice would eat Company C's chow—its mess sergeant, Sgt. Robinet, was an outstanding cook. Besides tastier food,

Rice got out of all work details while we had to take turns guarding him. But he did not bother anyone and was apparently content to give up comparative freedom for better chow, and did not mind solitude.

We had a small library at the camp of 1200 prisoners, but I was never able to take out a book. The officers and special duty men always got to the books while we were on work details in the morning, so none were left in the afternoon. Being on morning details also prevented me from attending classes in algebra, geometry, and German, because they were held only in the morning—I never knew why.

Our main work on morning details was not difficult. We tore down barracks at a former Philippine barracks nearby and walked the lumber back to Malaybalay—it was supposed to be used for construction. Unlike the guards at Camp Keithley, the Japanese did not invade our sleeping quarters for loot. The chow was good on the whole, and the climate at an altitude of 1800 feet was healthy. Everything was so nice and peaceful that one could forget he was a prisoner. But this situation did not last.

VIII

Transport to Japan

September 30, 1942, to November 12, 1942

We suspected that our good days at Malaybalay were coming to an end on September 6 when the Japs sent all of our colonels and generals to Manila. We believed they were to be questioned at Japanese Army HQ and then interned at Cabanatuan, a prison camp on Luzon. One of the generals was Guy Fort, our commanding officer at Lake Lanao. Somehow he had not been executed at Camp Keithley in retaliation for the escape of our four prisoners. But later he paid with his life for refusing to cooperate after the Japs took him back to Lake Lanao to help pacify the Moros. Fort's aide, our small friend Dick Beck, went to Manila with Fort but survived the war.

By September 15, the Japs had plans for the rest of the Americans. Those with technical skills were offered jobs and would be taken to Manila. There were 276 of us. I was promised a job in Manila as an aircraft technician. But some Americans were suspicious, and so claimed no skills. They were to go to the Davao Penal Colony—formerly a Philippine prison farm near the city of Davao on Mindanao. One who chose the prison farm was Vic Mapes. He was a farm boy and thought he would be happier at the prison farm. He was all right until September 1944 when he almost lost his life—he was being transported on an unmarked prison ship that was torpedoed by an American submarine. He and only 82 others out of the 750 prisoners on the *Shinyo Maru* survived—many prisoners had gotten off the ship, but Japs in small boats shot most of them in the water. Mapes' experience showed another instance when my choice—to have a skill rather than go to Davao—probably saved my life.

Mapes also remembers a gruesome incident that occurred at Malay-balay after my skilled group left on September 30. In the weeks that fol-lowed, the Japanese benevolence toward the Filipino prisoners there ended suddenly after two Filipinos tried to escape. The Japs tied them to posts and mustered all prisoners, American and Filipino, to witness the execu-tions. The Filipino soldiers faced their deaths with defiant faces before the firing squad riddled them with bullets. The Japs left them tied to the posts all day, as though the prisoners had not gotten the message.*

Those of us going to Manila were first trucked north to Cagayan, where we boarded the *Takahoma Maru* for transport to Manila. After an uneventful three-day voyage we docked at Pier 5 on October 5. It was dark before they finished hosing us down and spraying us for lice. Then we marched through the deserted streets of Manila to Bilibid Prison. It was a sad walk because we remembered how lively the city was the last time we had seen it. Now there were a few spots open, but the music com-ing out of them had a subdued and forced tone. The few people we saw wore defeated expressions and looked the other way as we passed by. We reached the prison at 11 P.M. and found places to sleep on the concrete floor.

In the morning, instead of being assigned technical jobs, we were told nothing. I wandered around the prison and was surprised to hear a voice that sounded like Paul Reuter, a 14th Squadron friend. He had been left on Bataan when most of the 14th Squadron had sailed for Mindanao. Now I turned around to greet a barely-living skeleton of 100 pounds or less—he had weighed 180 pounds when I last saw him. He said, "Hey, Herb, you're looking pretty good." I returned his greeting but couldn't say much because I was so shocked by his terrible-looking condition—I just knew he would never live long enough to get home.

Compared to our group from Malaybalay, the other POWs at Bili-bid Prison, like Paul Reuter, were skin and bones, and I believed their health had little chance to improve because of the poor food and hard work demanded of them. Then I visited the hospital cemetery and found many graves of Air Corps soldiers from our 19th Group who were left on Bataan to join the infantry there.

After two more nights on the concrete floor, any hope regarding the promises made to me at Malaybalay had gone down the drain. At dawn on October 8 we were ordered aboard the *Tottori Maru*, an old freighter converted into a troop ship. Besides the 276 of us from Malaybalay, 1800 Americans, who had been on the Death March from Bataan, were packed

*Mapes, The Butchers, the Baker, *page 172.*

in the two aft holds of the ship. One thousand Japanese troops easily fit into the two forward holds. But trying to jam the 2,000 Americans into the aft holds, intended for 500, was quite a feat. Yet with Jap guards pushing and cussing, it was accomplished. Of course, yours truly was on the bottom of the three sleeping levels. We were so tightly wedged in there was almost no room to lie down, so some had to sit. We found we were bound for Japan—a daunting journey of over 2,000 miles for us, even if we sailed a direct route to Tokyo.

The first thing I did was to eat all three loaves of the bread the Philippine Red Cross had given each of us before we boarded. I wanted to make sure that I did not lose the bread or have it stolen. I was glad I did because fights broke out later over bread that had not been eaten.

Late in the morning the *Tottori Maru* got underway. The early chill in the hold turned into unbearable heat because of the rising sun and heat from our bodies. I scrambled up to the main deck to get some air.

On deck, lines of POWs were making continual use of latrines on both sides of the ship. They were mostly prisoners from Cabanatuan—veterans of the Bataan Death March. They were suffering from acute diarrhea and did not dare stray from the latrine line.

The deck became so crowded that we had little space to stretch out. But the guards did not try to send us back into the rear holds. They were too busy jabbering among themselves and showing us the things they had looted from Filipinos. They were especially proud of the leather goods they had snatched—boots, knapsacks, and belts that were far superior to the cheap canvas equipment of the Japanese Army.

The first morning after sailing from Manila, I was sitting in the hold with gloomy thoughts of the future when loud whistles on deck jolted me back to the present. Then many footsteps pounded on the main deck above me, followed by random shots by the artillery pieces strapped on the aft deck and thumps as they recoiled. Tension built up in the hold. Then someone yelled down the hatch that we were being torpedoed.

Men scrambled madly for the ladder to the deck. When I saw that nobody in the panicked crowd was getting far, I sat down and thought, "To hell with it! I'll die just as dead on deck. Why should I fight to get there?" Now the ship began to rock like mad as the captain steered wildly in evasive action. Then some men yelled and others prayed to their gods— the Japanese louder than the Americans.

But I sat in the hold, strangely calm, and just waited to see what would happen. After the firing ceased and the ship steadied in the water,

Opposite: Route of *Tottori Maru* from Manila to Japan.

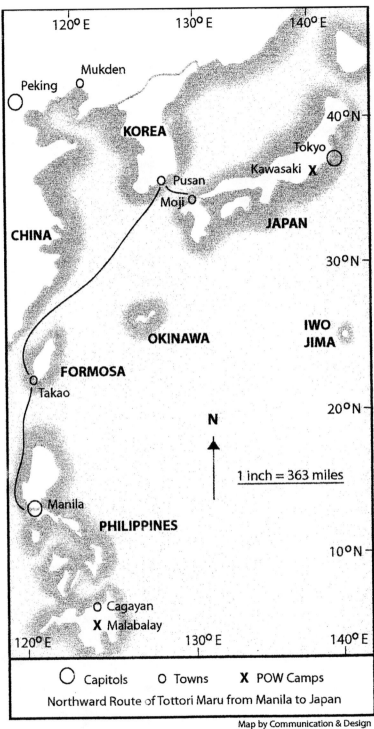

Northward Route of Tottori Maru from Manila to Japan

things calmed down. I learned that a torpedo had been fired at us, but it had "broken water" early and missed. Later an American sailor told me that our submarine was using a new type of torpedo that didn't work right—otherwise we would have been hit and probably sunk.* It was yet another of my close calls. U.S. attacks on the unmarked prison ships probably accounted for most of the 10,853 POWs who drowned enroute to prison camps—a large proportion of the 55,279 who were shipped.†

On October 11, two days after the torpedo attack, we anchored outside the harbor of Takao (now Kaohsiung) on the southwest coast of Formosa (now Taiwan). The devastating attack on Clark Field at the war's beginning had been launched from Formosa. The next day we passed through the fortified natural entrance into the protected harbor.

In the following days the Malaybalay prisoners noticed that the men from Cabanatuan—who had been on the Bataan Death March—were always talking about how much they hated General Douglas MacArthur and, to a lesser degree, all officers on Bataan (who were blamed for getting the men into a hopeless situation). The few American officers from Cabanatuan stayed away from the Bataan enlisted men—always on a different side of the ship. Even so, the men snarled insults at the officers— only the more seasoned soldiers stopped the men from rioting. Our Malaybalay group did not have a generalized anti-officer attitude.

The Cabanatuan men fought and re-fought the battles on Bataan and Corregidor to the last detail. They told how the "brass" had burned up food depots while the men on the front lines were on half rations of rice. I could understand their bitterness. The Bataan veterans would never forget the many instances of mismanagement and stupidity.

One of the Cabanatuan officers, Major Hankins, was the most rotten man I'd ever come across. He buddied up to the Japanese and got permission to sell some Philippine sugar he had brought aboard. He had six 100-pound sacks stacked on the deck next to the latrine and sold small amounts of this filthy, vermin-infested sugar to his own soldiers for American or Japanese money. I hope Hankins choked on whatever money he made—the men who ate it probably died of dysentery later.

Fortunately I had no money so bought none of the sugar. I suffered from diarrhea but am reasonably certain I did not get dysentery. However, it was a continual struggle for me to keep clean because of the crowded conditions and lack of showers. I became somewhat of a fanatic

---

*The last defects of the prewar Mark 14 torpedo were not eliminated until September 1943.

†Linda G. Holmes, Unjust Enrichment (Stackpole, 2001), page 33.

about cleanliness—trading many non-essential items to Japanese soldiers for poor-quality soap. Even so, I probably stank to high heaven. Except for diarrhea I had no disease. Although I lost 10 to 15 pounds, I still weighed about 150 pounds and stayed in better health than most prisoners on the "Torture Maru," as we called the ship. But the cases of diarrhea and dysentery among the rest of the prisoners had increased greatly—even among the healthier Malaybalay prisoners who had lost much of their resistance by then.

On October 12, 1942, we passed through the heavily-guarded natural entrance to the enclosed harbor of Takao on the southwest coast of Formosa, now Taiwan. Two days later, barges pulled alongside to load us with food supplies. We received large amounts of rice, potatoes, cucumbers, onions, meat, fish, and 620 cases of Japanese Army hardtack or crackers. Five hundred Japanese soldiers also came aboard, but all we cared about was the food. But the soldiers probably ate a good share of the fresh food because the variety and quality of our meals picked up for only a few days. After that we were on crackers and thin soup for each meal.

On October 16 we sailed from Takao but turned back after dark and were again in Takao by 10:30 P.M. It was said that American submarines had caused us to return. The next day, inside the harbor, we joined a group of freighters that carried Japanese soldiers. The following day at 7:30 A.M. we sailed from Takao as part of the troop convoy. But we soon anchored off an island, said to be Bogota, and stayed there for nine days. During this time I was a member of the burial crew.

Surprisingly, there were only seven deaths during my stint. We sewed the body in a burlap sack, laid it on a board, and covered it with an American flag. After an officer spoke a few words, we lifted the board to the railing, removed the flag to use again, and tilted the board—sending another good soldier to the depths of the sea. I doubt that any record was kept of the deceased. The dead soldier's personal effects usually were given to his closest buddy.

On October 27 we got underway at dawn and returned with the convoy to Takao and anchored. At dusk we were glad to see provision barges draw alongside and start to unload—it had been at least a week since we had eaten any of the food brought aboard on October 14. Two days later the *Tottori Maru* tied up at the dock, where the guards lined us up for hosing down. Japanese doctors gave us a dysentery smear, but no one ever learned whether he tested positive or negative. I doubt whether anything would have been done if dysentery had been detected. The guards said the ship had been fumigated while we were on the dock. But when we boarded again, the hold smelled as filthy as ever, so I kept on sleeping on the deck.

The next day we slipped out of Takao at dawn—this time without convoy. In the afternoon we were at Bogota again, where we had two meals of rice, one bag of crackers, and a cup of tea. We saw no more of the fresh provisions that were loaded on October 27.

The following morning we headed north from Bogota. Living conditions below deck had become so bad that my friend Sgt. Lubiewski and I commandeered a spot for sleeping between two winches on the aft deck. It was probably as dirty as in the hold, but it was warmer, the air was fresh, and we didn't have to struggle against others to stretch out. One of us stayed at our spot at all times, or we would have lost it. But two days later, on November 2, it became pretty cold on deck as we sailed north and winter approached. But we didn't move because of the crowded, smelly hold. The same day we watched the Nips practice gunnery with their antiquated 3-inch gun mounted on the deck—they couldn't hit the broad side of a barn.

The following day two Nip sailors died—one of dysentery and one of malaria. A couple of days later two American soldiers and one marine died of dysentery—probably from Major Hankins' sugar.

On November 7 we docked in the harbor of Pusan on the southeast coast of Korea—the peninsula of Korea was a Japanese colony. The port city looked cold and dismal—like the weather during the past few days. The next morning the Nips took 1,000 survivors of the Bataan Death March off the ship and made them strip down on the dock. It was terribly cold under a dark sky, but the Japanese doctors took their time, poking the prisoners' stomachs and looking in their mouths. These men, considerably weaker than our group from Malaybalay, were being sent farther north to prison camps in Mukden in Manchuria*—a province the Japs had taken in their decade-long war with China.

The prisoners going to Manchuria did get some warm clothing, but on the ship our khaki shorts and short-sleeved shirts did not keep us warm. When we asked for warmer clothes, they told us, "You're going to Japan so you won't need heavy clothes—it doesn't get cold there." This didn't make much sense because Pusan and Tokyo are at the same latitude. It was so cold that Lubiewski and I planned to abandon our sleeping spot on deck for the hold.

When it became dark, we slipped out of Pusan's harbor. Lubiewski and I noticed that the Nips were all wearing lifebelts for the first time—worrying about American submarines operating in the Sea of Japan. Ed

---

*POW Ken Towery began work at the Mitsubishi complex in Mukden in early 1942. Of the 920 who came on his prison ship, 300 died the first winter. See Holmes, Unjust Enrichment, page 9.

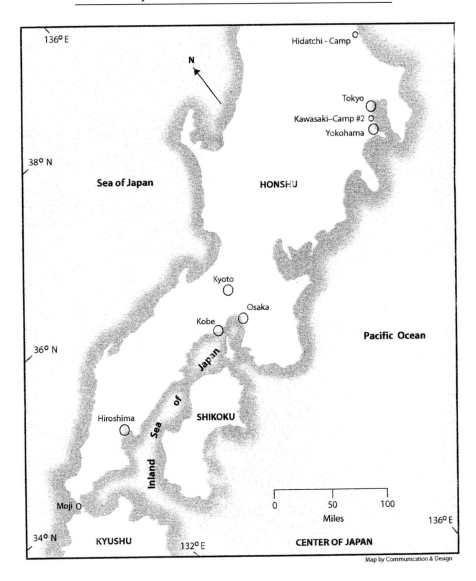

Center of Japan

and I changed our minds about sleeping in the hold and stayed on deck. We weren't alone—both Japanese and Americans stayed topside as our old freighter headed into the darkness at full steam. No one dared to go below, despite the cold wind—one Nip sailor died of the cold during the night. But he was not slipped over the side until dawn when we anchored outside Moji, a port on Kyushu—Japan's southernmost main island.

We stayed only long enough for to us to strip on the deck so doctors from the port could have their fun poking us and take more dysentery smears. Then we got underway for passage through the Inland Sea of Japan, just as one more Marine died of dysentery. With us nearing our destination in Japan, the Nips ordered everyone to get haircuts and shave. It was hard to find enough scissors and razors, but finally prisoners who had them lent theirs to those without. We took turns cutting each other's hair and sometimes shaving one another in the absence of enough mirrors. After losing our beards and long hair, we felt the cold weather even more. However, we were ordered into the warmer holds for passage through Japan's Inland Sea to Osaka. The Japs didn't want us to see their military installations—as though we had any way to report something of interest to American intelligence.

On November 11 we docked at Osaka and came out of the holds to the coldest weather yet—the Japs were nuts in claiming it didn't get cold in Japan. We had been below deck while the old freighter steamed 250 miles from the southern to the northern end of the Inland Sea. At 1 P.M. we stepped off the *Tottori Maru* for good and lined up on the dock. Then we marched two miles to the railroad yards. After doctors or someone examined our throats, we began the coldest damn wait I have ever known. Ice was on the ground, but we were wearing khaki tropical uniforms. I couldn't find Lubiewski but huddled under a blanket with M/Sgt. Tom Wyllsey, the crew chief on the B-17 I armed at Clark Field. But we just shivered together instead of separately.

After four hours the train finally came, but only 70 of us got aboard, while 70 were left to shiver. On boarding, we were given a box lunch of rice, one small fried fish, and pickled dikons, which were like white radishes. As we traveled through the night, they had us draw the blinds—to keep us and Japanese civilians from seeing each other, to keep us from seeing military installations, or to protect us from Japanese civilians?

IX

In the Care of Doc Curtin, Porky, and a Guard

November 12, 1942, to April 20, 1943

In the early light of November 12, I could see Mount Fujiyama through the blinds of our train, even though they had been drawn—to keep us from learning any secrets from observing Japanese installations. The snow-capped Fujiyama made me feel colder than ever—we had not warmed up overnight on the unheated train after our four-and-a-half-hour wait in freezing weather at the Osaka station the day before. All morning we continued northeast past Fujiyama before debarking at 1:30 P.M. at Yokohama—a run of almost 300 miles from Osaka. At the Yokohama station they herded us onto another train for a short trip to Kawasaki.

From the Kawasaki station, the guards marched us through a heavy industrial area while I began to feel more and more pain in my left heel. A blister that formed during the all-day July 4 march on Mindanao (conducted to punish us for the escape of four prisoners) had never healed. Now, I did not complain or slow up because the Japs just shot the prisoners who had not been able to keep up during that march. So I kept going but was limping badly by the time we came to a halt after a three-mile hike from the station.

The guards lined the 300 of us up in a small yard across the street from a two-story stucco building. Next, a Nip officer gave us a "pep" talk. The interpreter could not speak very good English, but the gist of the talk was, "You are not prisoners of war but guests of the Emperor. Nevertheless, do

71

not try to escape or you will be shotted!" After that cheery speech, we were given numbers—I became number 393. Then they issued us two heavy blankets, two light ones, and three China eating bowls of various sizes. The blankets were of poor-grade cotton, but we were surprised and grateful to receive them.

Then the guards directed us across the street and into the stucco building, which had been converted into a barracks from an office building. Carpenters had built sleeping shelves on both sides of a center aisle on each floor. The lower shelf was a foot and a half off the floor—a simple, wood platform covered by a thin grass matting. The top sleeping shelf was six feet above the lower one and was reached by a crude ladder. I chose a top shelf. But it was hard to undress because I was so near the ceiling I couldn't get off my knees. The difficulty of climbing up and down the ladder to go to the latrine was another bad feature of my choice.

As we settled in, we didn't realized that our Camp No. 2 at Kawasaki was one of 127 POW camps in Japan—urgently needed by Japanese

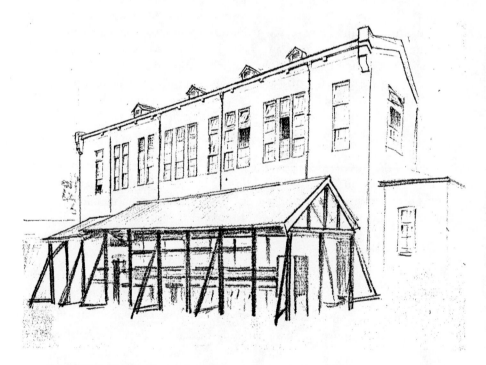

Camp No. 2, Kawasaki—washracks for mess gear in front. (Courtesy of William H. Thomas)

industry for wartime production.* Our barracks belonged to the large Mitsui Corporation; it owned and operated the nearby docks and many of the factories around us.

The morning after our arrival we filled out forms that called for our name, serial number, rank, organization, and nationality. In the afternoon we had to strip in the unheated barracks while a grinning Nip medical corporal poked our skinny bodies as though he knew what he was doing. His name was Watanabe, but when he wasn't around, we came to call him Porky because of his chubbiness.

The following day the guards inspected our personal equipment and confiscated much of it. They took our razors and knives and gave them to our officers for safekeeping. But these items were returned when the camp commander decided there was no chance of their being used as weapons. But nobody shaved—partly because beards were thought to help keep us warm. That night the Nips must have been busy because the next morning they posted a list of the personal belongings that they had taken from us. In the afternoon we learned to count in Japanese to make roll call easy for the guards. So the next day the first prisoner started with "one" in Japanese, and the rest of us continued until the last one ended with the final number—telling the Nips if we were all there or not. They also made it clear how we should line up, and how to salute and bow in true Japanese style.

On November 16 the commandant of Tokyo POW camps inspected us—at Kawasaki we were on Tokyo Bay just south of Tokyo and just north of Yokohama. There was much bowing and hissing by the lower-ranked Nips on the camp staff in the presence of this high-ranking officer. He must have been a colonel or general—we could not yet tell rank from their collar insignia. We must have made a good showing because the commandant didn't give any of the Japs or us a hard time—or else he didn't give a damn.

Although we had blankets for sleeping, we still had only tropical clothing to wear. We constantly complained, and they finally issued each of us a British Army blouse, trousers, long-johns, and heavy shoes. This clothing was said to have been taken from the British after their surrender at Singapore. Though of rough material, these clothes were a blessing in the cold weather. But the new shoes did not help because my infected left foot had swollen so I couldn't get my shoe on. The next day Cpl. Watanabe gave us a mouth and chest examination, but we never knew if Porky found anything.

*Holmes, Unjust Enrichment, *page 25.*

There was a lot of idle time during these five days of inspections and instructions. We talked about American food we had eaten in the past and would eat in the future—if things worked out right. But I learned not to indulge in such bull sessions. To aggravate our hunger with verbal pictures of steaks and cakes could drive one to near-insanity or self-pity because the contrast with current reality was too great.

Finally, on November 18, the guards took us out for our first day's work in the factories. They fixed me up with a Japanese wooden shoe that reached over my swollen left foot. Some of us went to Kosaka Soko, a plant of the Showa Denko Chemical Works. The guards stayed with us as though we were about to escape. But we would have been fools to try anything with nowhere to go and no knowledge of the language. Our work at the factory was hard but simple—merely moving dirt and trash from one place to another. Yet it was a welcome change from lying around camp talking about food we might never enjoy.

Though we began to work every day, our diet continued to be bad. We had boiled rice with daikon* and miso† three times a day. Even though it was boring, there was not enough of it. The inexperienced American cooks always left some burnt rice in the cooking vats. Rations were so small, however, that everyone wanted his tiny share of the burnt rice. But some were always left out. There were lots of complaints until it was decided to dispense the burnt rice by the 12-man sections into which we were divided in the barracks. Although the burnt rice reaching each man was of little nutritional value, the bickering stopped and morale improved.

I put in seven days of hard work at Kosaka Soko while my left foot stayed swollen because of beriberi—an ailment that commonly results when polished rice is the main part of the diet. Yet what brought me down was yellow jaundice—everything looked yellow to me and I felt weak as a kitten. Moreover, I could not keep anything in my stomach—a dangerous situation since I needed every grain of rice to keep going. Now Porky gave me a pot of green tea and let me go to bed for a few days. But in a day or two my appetite came back—the green tea may have helped.

Yet my beriberi had become worse. Both legs were now swollen from knees to feet, and they felt like lead weights. To walk was a great effort— I felt like I was walking on pins and needles. Others had a touch of beriberi, but I had an advanced case. Nevertheless, on December 9, after recovering from yellow jaundice, I volunteered to work on the Mitsui work detail

*A white vegetable, a cross between a radish and a turnip with practically no flavor.
†A brown paste that is the final dregs of the mashed soy bean after everything else has been extracted—it tasted like what it looked like.

that unloaded coal ships. I was eager to do something different. But my legs were so weak I had to pull myself by the arms to get up and down the ship's gangplank. I could shovel coal OK by standing still and putting most of my weight on the shovel. But I had to be helped on and off the ship while listening to the taunts of some who thought I was "gold-bricking." The next day Porky let me stay in because of my legs.

But my beriberi made me feel so exhausted I wanted to stay in bed all day. As I lay there, comfortable and glad not to be working, a low-ranking Jap guard, probably a private, jabbed me with his bayonet. Startled, I wondered what I had done. The guard did not snarl but ordered, "Get up. Start moving." I was afraid not to obey but silently swore at him as I got up. Then I hobbled aimlessly around with swollen legs and feet that were pricked with needles at every step. But the guard showed no mercy and kept me out of the sack. But, unbelievably, after an hour or so I had the strong urge to urinate. I discharged copious quantities of liquid from my bloated body. Then I no longer felt the dangerous lassitude that is the fatal stage for beriberi patients.

In the next few days I looked for the guard who had saved my life. He was jabbering with two or three of his buddies and barely acknowledge my thanks with a gruff, "OK. OK. OK." He may have been afraid of losing face with his buddies if he seemed friendly with a POW.

I was discussing my condition with "Blackie" Young later that day when we heard the angry shouts of "Bucktooth" Kasuya, the Jap quartermaster. Some prisoner had annoyed him, so Bucktooth made the culprit slap another prisoner. But when that blow did not floor or make the innocent victim bleed, Bucktooth became furious—the blow against a fellow prisoner had been pulled, of course.

Now Bucktooth called us all downstairs and lined us up in two rows, facing each other. After demonstrating how we should hit each other, he had us slap each other for a half-hour—each row taking turns at slapping and receiving blows. If someone seemed to be holding back, Bucktooth stepped in and showed how he wanted it done. He was a big half–Mongolian and could really clip a man. I was good-sized, but my slapping partner, Blackie Young, was larger. Nevertheless, we must have put on a good demonstration because Bucktooth did not notice how easy we had been on each other. Our faces were flushed, but neither of us had broken skin or bones. My swollen legs seemed to be none the worse, and maybe the exercise was good for me. When Bucktooth had finally finished with us, someone came up with a name for our barracks—the Mitsui Madhouse.

I had not been a close friend of Blackie, but he must have trusted me after our performance in front of Bucktooth. A few days later he asked if

I wanted to have some extra rice. I would earn it by joining with him in a scheme he had worked out. He had the job of crane operator on a work detail and had installed a hot plate in his cab that one of the men had stolen—the Japs at the factory never checked inside the crane's cab. The prisoners on work details were always on the lookout for rice to steal, and had achieved some success. They delivered the rice to Blackie, who hid it in his clothes when he went to work. While operating the crane, Blackie cooked the rice on the hot plate. Later he secured the cooked rice under his belt and brought it into the barracks. I was in the hospital section and less apt to be searched, so Blackie asked me to act as a storage location until the cooked rice could be distributed to members of the rice conspiracy.

I was very receptive to Blackie's offer because of the Japanese Army policy of putting sick POWs, as well as their own sick soldiers, on half-rations when not working—they weren't earning a full ration. This policy discouraged "gold-bricking," but it was an endless struggle for the truly sick to maintain strength, let alone recover. The only exception for POWs would be an injury suffered at a factory that was determined to have been the factory's fault.

One afternoon Blackie had delivered some cooked rice to me in small sacks as usual. But the rice had not been picked up when I went to sleep that night, so I kept it by my side on the sleeping shelf. Sometime in the night I was aroused by someone climbing up the six-foot ladder to my bunking space. Conscious of my rice sacks, I had just rolled over on top of them when I recognized the leading Jap noncom, Sgt. Shiozawa, as he scrambled off the ladder. He looked at me without much interest, said "Pardon," and proceeded to search through all my belongings while I sweated blood. Finally he climbed back down the ladder—having taken nothing and none the wiser about the rice. The next day I resigned from the rice conspiracy.

On December 11 Porky gave me a shot in the arm and some powder for my beriberi—the powder, said to be ground-up rice husks, may have had some vitamin B value. Porky gave me another shot three days later while the Chief Medical Inspector for Tokyo inspected us. Porky wanted to show that he was doing something for my beriberi. The stocky Inspector was a puzzle because he wore no ribbons or braid like other high-ranking officers. The next day a Swiss Red Cross representative visited us. Many Japanese officers accompanied him, and as he walked along he looked like he wanted to stop and talk to us. But the officers kept him moving along—he seemed to be almost as much a prisoner as we were.

Discouraged by the Red Cross inspection, and with my foot still painful, I asked George Nuzzo, a medic from the 60th Coast Artillery, to look at my infected and swollen left heel. He sterilized the blade of his pocket knife and cut a two-inch slice on the side of my heel. The yellow pus gushed out like a fountain, and the relief from the throbbing pain was almost immediate. After Nuzzo bound up the wound with bandages and gauze, I had my first decent night's sleep in weeks, despite the colder weather, which made the unheated barracks feel like an ice box.

To keep warm inside, we wore all our clothing plus a blanket or two over our shoulders and sat together in a huddle for body heat. Yet the guards said it was not officially winter until January 1 when the Emperor would decree it! Then they would light up the stoves. On December 18, however, they installed three coal stoves upstairs and three downstairs, but lit no fires. Nevertheless, we huddled around the stoves and held our hands over the imaginary heat.

M/Sgt. F. M. Stansell didn't make it to Christmas of 1942—dying of pneumonia and malnutrition during the night of December 22. I felt his loss particularly because he had been the flight crew chief of one of the B-17 bombers that I was responsible for arming at Clark Field.

We had been told that we wouldn't go on work details on Christmas, but didn't expect anything else. So we were pleasantly surprised when the guards brought out boxes from the British Red Cross. There was a box for each man, which contained cans of condensed milk, stewed beef, apple pudding, cheese, and jam, as well as granulated sugar, a fourth of a choco-late bar, and soap. The Japs added an apple, tangerine, and a pack of cig-arettes for each man. Everyone had a lot of fun trading for what he liked most in the assortment. One fellow, however, traded everything else in his box for milk, sugar, and jam, then mixed it in a large bowl. After devouring the whole thing, he suffered the most vicious case of diarrhea for a week. I thought he might die. I traded away only my bar of soap and cigarettes. That food package was a wonderful gift—it gave us a new lease on life. Dinner was also something to celebrate—we had a loaf of bread and a thick stew of pork, carrots, onions, white potatoes, beans, and cab-bage. For dessert there was chocolate pudding. We hadn't eaten so much since the start of the war—a little more than a year before. We all made hogs of ourselves. I was no exception, and had the wonderful, satisfied feel-ing of a full stomach.

By December 29 my beriberi had improved enough for Porky to send me out to work. My detail went to a railroad yard, where I enjoyed the hard work of lifting and laying new rails. Then for a day I shoveled coal in the hold of a ship again before going back to laying rails.

But in a few days my heel became infected and swollen again, so I had to change back to my wooden shoe. On January 10 George Nuzzo lanced my heel again. This time the relief was only temporary, and Nuzzo told me I needed help. By January 13 the pain was killing me. As I lay helpless on my sleeping shelf, I heard Porky and a superior from outside the camp talking about my case. They had decided to send me to Shinagawa Hospital for treatment—where all the very sick POWs were sent. I thought this would be a good idea since I was just getting worse where I was. But I heard someone with a British accent break in, "You don't need to send him to Shinagawa. I'll take care of him so he won't be a burden here." Porky and his boss agreed with the Britisher and walked away, leaving the Britisher with me. Then I looked at his neat uniform and realized he was Lt. Peter Curtin, a captured British Navy doctor who had entered Camp No. 2 the day before.

Not happy about not being sent to the hospital for treatment, I asked the doctor, "Why did you do that?" Curtin answered, "I know that hospital. They would just chop off your foot, and infection could very well lead to more amputations. That could be the end of you." I could only reply, "I'm with you, doctor. Take care of me."* He started by cleaning my foot with alcohol after cutting away the rotten flesh—leaving my whole heel bared almost to the bone. It hurt like hell, but I was now confident I was in the hands of a doctor who knew what he was doing.

Doc Curtin had been informed of my condition by George Nuzzo, the medic POW who had lanced my heel. Then Curtin had taken me as his first case after being assigned medical work at the camp. He was of very low rank in the British Navy—a member of the Royal Navy Volunteer Reserve, which is practically the bottom of the ladder at the Admiralty in London. But for my money, and that of the other men in this camp, he was a life-saver. He treated all of us at one time or another for everything from broken limbs to malaria or the diseases resulting from dietary deficiencies. In our rundown condition a minor scratch could develop into something serious—I was a good example, because my bad foot started with a blister I developed on our Mindanao march on July 4

---

*Dr. Curtin's opinion of Shinagawa Hospital must have come from earlier dealings with it when he was in another camp of POWs. The postwar War Crimes Tribunal in Yokohama tried Shinagawa's wartime director, Dr. Hisakichi Tokuda, and convicted him of causing the death of four POWs and hastening the death of another by intravenous injections of soybean milk—apparently his idea of an experiment was to modify the orthodox procedure of oral ingestion. He kept on trying this procedure even after fatalities occurred. He was sentenced to death by hanging, but General MacArthur commuted the sentence to life imprisonment. As a result, Tokuda was in line to have been released by 1958 when all Japanese were pardoned and let go. John L. Ginn, Sugamo Prison, Tokyo (McFarland, 1992), pages 87ff.

of last year. I didn't think much about it at the time, but it had never healed.

Doc Curtin, always neatly dressed in his British officers' uniform, was in almost continuous conflict with the Japanese staff over keeping sick prisoners off work details. His insistence on these cases caused the Japs to beat him from time to time—sometimes by swatting him about the head with his own shoes. But they were careful not to injure him badly—probably having a British doctor made the guard staff look good during the frequent inspections by senior Army officers. Curtin did succeed in establishing a separate hospital area for sick prisoners such as myself.

On the evening of January 23, Lt. Myazaki drank quite a bit of sake and then walked up to a prisoner and gave him a cigarette. After making a few friendly remarks in broken English, the lieutenant turned on his heel and went back to his office. But in a moment, Myazaki roared back into the barracks, lined us up and began slapping everyone. The prisoner's failure to bow upon receiving the cigarette had infuriated him. Then the tipsy officer turned loose the camp guards on us to continue the beatings. After they had finished, the Japanese insisted that we bow and thank them. We nicknamed Lt. Myazaki "Little Henry" because of his small size and baby face, which made us think of the comic-strip character. Little Henry didn't look as mean as the guards, but had more authority and treated us worse, as well as being unpredictable.

Sgt. Shiozawa, Lt. Myazaki, Cpl. Watenaabe, Bucktooth Kasuya—we came under their control at Camp No. 2, Kawasaki. (Courtesy, Edward Jackfert)

It was very hard to take such beatings and not fight back. Yet when one of the prisoners seemed about to boil over, "Stinky" Maniere of our mess crew would make a joking remark about these "slant-eyed" Japs and break the tension—luckily, the interpreter wasn't around to hear the insult. Stinky, whose nickname was derived from his last name, was a likeable, unassuming sailor. Over the years in that camp, Stinky and others intervened to help anyone keep his head who was about to lose his temper and risk a severe beating, if not his life.

On January 25, Oliver W. Krueger of the 14th Bomb Squadron died of stomach ulcers. He could keep nothing down, although we all donated some of our remaining Red Cross food—hoping he could hold it. He was well-liked and a great loss to me because he was a close friend.

At the end of January, Little Henry jumped on us again over a minor incident. We were learning to avoid talking with him or the guards—they might notice or manipulate some infraction of their rules. Then that could justify punishment of all of us.

Since most of us had been taken in the Philippines, we were probably the objects of particular bitterness. The American and Filipino soldiers on Bataan had cost the Japanese 10,000 casualties and five months of combat.* Yet we were also the objects of contempt because we had surrendered—not a normal or honorable course for a Japanese soldier.

Because of the hate and contempt, the guards didn't even need a pretext to invade our barracks after lights were out. They would turn them back on and stomp around our bunk shelves, looking for girlie pictures. They liked the nude ones the best. During regular hours such pictures could be soap or money. Sometimes guards came in at night simply to steal personal pictures, letters, and other items. We complained to our officers, who talked to the camp commander, a lieutenant. But the looting continued for months before it finally died out.

I escaped this stomping around at night because Doc Curtin still had me in the hospital section—the guards stayed out because they were afraid of catching something. When they did venture in, they wore white rubber gloves and nose masks. That made them look almost intelligent.

In February a Red Cross radio with loudspeaker came, but we would have been better off without it. The Japs kept it in their office and turned the loudspeaker way up so we had to hear Japanese jabbering or horrible Japanese music all day and half the night.

The Red Cross also sent us records, some books, and a copy of *Mainichi*, a daily newspaper. It was translated into English but was so full

*Homes, Unjust Enrichment, *page 17.*

of propaganda that it was difficult to learn how the war was going. But Commander Loojen, the tall, lanky Dutch submarine skipper with a black moustache, had brought maps of the southwest Pacific with him.* He located Guadalcanal on his maps—from where the Japs were claiming a clever withdrawal. We later learned that American forces secured Guadalcanal on February 14—the first American ground victory of the war, which stopped Japanese forces short of Australia.

But it was rare to find an English translation of the newspapers. Yet a solution evolved, as two Americans, Sgt. William McCool and Pfc. Oliver Gilbert, began to teach themselves to speak and read Japanese. We passed any newspapers we found to either one of them, hoping they could make something out of the bizarre letters. Now Commander Loojen and his maps helped again. When McCool and Gilbert had some confusing information, they would slip into Loojen's quarters. There the three of them would digest the Japanese press reports. Later, by word of mouth, the whole camp would be informed of the gradual retreat of the Japanese war machine.

The food orgy of Christmas Day was a one-time occasion. By early February 1943, our skimpy diet of rice and soup (of mostly clear water with stray daikons) was taking a greater toll. Two men were sent to Shinagawa Hospital because of uncontrollable diarrhea—we were all bothered by it, but some worse than others. After a general physical on February 7, the men with dysentery were moved to the first floor to be closer to the outdoor latrine. Then two men were brought back from work details after collapsing on the job. Everyone was losing weight because of the small ration of poor food. I was able to survive on the half-rations in the hospital section because Blackie persuaded me to rejoin the rice conspiracy. Later in the month Porky gave me a jar of beriberi powder. Doc Curtin had obtained a quantity of it and told me, "It can't hurt you, and it might do some good."

In mid–February they began feeding us barley instead of rice. The greater bulk was welcome; but there were stomach cramps, and gas stunk up the barracks at night. Then we had a couple of good meals of barley that was mixed with carrots, onions, turnips, and pork.

On February 24 the camp paid me 90 sen for working from December 26 to January 31—my pay was not reduced for being in the hospital section most of that time. Our pay was supposed to be based on four yen per day. But all of that was taken out for food, quarters, and clothing,

---

*Commander Loojen had been a submarine skipper who had been taken by a German raider and turned over to Japan.

except for 10 sen per day for privates and 15 sen, or about 5 cents, per day for me and other NCOs. Officers got 25 sen per day, even if they chose not to work. Yet many officers worked to break the monotony.* The only place to spend the money was at a small PX at the camp. At this time I bought a can of fish powder. It was salty and added some taste to the rice and barley.

As mentioned, the guards stayed out of the hospital section because they feared germs. Yet after March 1 there was another advantage of my being there with my bad heel. March 1 was the date decreed by the Emperor to be the beginning of spring. In compliance, the Camp Commander had shut down all the stoves in the barracks—no matter that it was still damn cold. The next morning, Doc Curtin, immaculate in his uniform as usual, visited the camp commander. The stove in the hospital section was relit— a big comfort to me and the rest of the patients.

With the stove working in the hospital section, we could continue to cook the pilfered raw rice that the men were bringing in from work details—a better system than having Blackie Young cook the rice on the hot plate on his crane and then bringing it back for distribution. The adept pilferers wore two pairs of trousers and tied the under-pair at the calf with leggings. At the warehouses the rice thief would lean against a pile of rice sacks and stick a sharpened piece of hollow bamboo into a sack. Then he pushed the other end of the bamboo under his belt so the rice could run inside his inner trousers. The men soon learned just how much they could carry back and get inside the barracks without having to walk stiff-legged. But on March 4 a guard spotted a pair of fat legs as the workers came back into the barracks. Then the guards looked more closely and found a few others. All of those caught were beaten. But many rice thieves continued to operate successfully.

Despite the pilfered rice, our men at Camp No. 2 were still losing weight and dying from malnutrition or the resulting inability to fend off beriberi, dysentery, malaria, and diarrhea. By mid–March, 1943, my weight had dropped to 146 pounds, as compared to 180 when we surrendered 10 months before on Mindanao.

Then on March 13 the food shortage resulted in a terrible conse-quence. At 2 A.M. the guards ordered everyone up. That included the hospital section, but we had to stay where we were. Nevertheless, we soon learned that a guard had caught a husky Marine, Don Armstrong,

---

*After the war it was found that many of the 158 other POW camps in Japan, the Philip-pines and elsewhere did not give the officers the option of not working. Holmes, Unjust Enrichment, page 25.

stealing bread from the galley. He had done it before and been caught, so the guards were in an angry mood. The sergeant of the guard, Shiozawa, first listened impatiently to Armstrong before calling in the American mess sergeant, Richard P. Hough, to inflict the punishment. Hough beat Armstrong, but hard—to the shock and disgust of all the men. Hough did not attempt to "pull his punches" and took full advantage of the fact that the guards saw to it that Armstrong did not fight back. Doc Curtin noticed what was happening and tried to intercede, but the guards told him to mind his own business—that the prisoners were subject to Japanese Army regulations. Violation of them meant punishment in the Japanese manner. Armstrong was thoroughly and unmercifully beaten to a pulp.

Everyone in the barracks except the hospital section was required to watch the beating—an example to keep us all in line. The hospital group learned later that when Armstrong was brought back to consciousness for the second time, he told Hough, "If I live through this prison camp, I'll kill you for this!" When Hough got through with Armstrong, he was taken by the Japs out to the guard house at the gate and then really "worked over" until after dawn. Then he was allowed to be helped to the barracks for breakfast. He was a rugged man, and he managed to drag himself up the stairs to his bunk. His face was blown up to three times its normal size, and his face was so swollen he could barely see.

Later in the day everyone suffering from diarrhea was given a shot. That shot had me on the run all night and the next day. After counting 50 trips to the latrine, I lost track. Sometimes it was "nip and tuck" to get back to the latrine when I hadn't even made it back to my bunk yet. What the hell did they have in that shot? Dynamite? But a week later our trips to the latrine had been reduced for most of us to the level during the early weeks at the camp in late 1942.

On March 17 Cpl. Henry B. Clements of the Marines died of malnutrition, but he brought it on himself. Not liking rice, he had traded it off in advance for the next ration of bread. But that was too long a wait because bread was seldom received in place of rice. When bread came, he would get a dozen loaves but could not space out his supply satisfactorily until bread again was served in the uncertain future. Over time, this poor planning, plus Clements' continual dreaming and talking of cake, ice cream, and other goodies that we all missed, was too much for him to handle. Another partly mental casualty a month later was Cpl. Robert A. Jammer, who died of pleurisy, diarrhea, and self-pity. He continually talked of his large bank account at home and bemoaned the fact that he couldn't even buy a candy bar now.

Pvt. H. G. Buelow of my 14th Squadron slept in the bunk space below me. In early April beriberi began to build up liquid in his body. Because of my experience with it, I noticed he was lapsing into a state of dangerous euphoria as he lay under me in the hospital section. I couldn't arouse him even by telling him of my own experience with beriberi on December 10 when a guard jabbed me with a bayonet and forced me to get up and move about. That guard saved my life, but Buelow wouldn't budge out of his sack and died on April 14.

The next day my weight was down again to 141 pounds, but on April 20 Doc Curtin moved me back with the healthy prisoners. I had been in the hospital section with my bad heel since January 10. before then my heel, plus beriberi, had kept me from working since December 10 except for a few days. Now I was able to take a full bath in the bath house for the first time in 1943. I no longer had to stand next to the tub to wash my body so as to keep my bad foot dry.

X

Master Sergeant Shiozawa

April 20, 1943, to September 16, 1943

The Jap guards and their NCOs worried themselves sick getting ready for an inspection of Camp No. 2 on May 8. After the general arrived, there was much bowing, scraping, and saluting. But all their preparation and pandering did them no good. When the inspection party came upon evidence of some prisoners' gambling, the general gave the camp commander a good swat, who in turn gave Shiozawa, the top NCO, a vigorous blow. Shiozawa never held back in swatting us and now beat his NCOs with equal vigor. The NCOs then rained blows on the guards, down to the lowliest private. By 9:30 A.M., the punishment reached the prisoners.

We had to stand at attention for an hour and a half, but the Japanese had an extreme meaning for "standing at attention"—arms stiffly at the sides, fingers extended down and joined, neck stiff, and eyes straight ahead without blinking. The guards stood at the head of each column and watched for a relaxed muscle or a blinking eye. Many failed to satisfy this scrutiny and were pulled out, tossed around in jiu-jitsu style, and then beat up a bit before being put back in the column. Although it was quite a strain, I managed to survive the hour and a half without being pulled out, even though I was tempted to ease my aching muscles and take the consequences. After that experience, all of us tried to rest up, if possible, the day before an inspection.

The next morning, while the men were waiting to go to work, Sgt. Shiozawa casually walked over to my friend Ed Lubiewski, who was sitting on his lower bunk. Shiozawa seemed relaxed, despite the poor camp inspection the day before—he gave Ed a cigarette and lit it for him. They smoked and chatted for awhile before the top Jap NCO went back to his office. But in a second Shiozawa came back scowling and pointed to the ashtray in the aisle by Ed's bunk. Then the sergeant seized a wooden slipper and whacked Ed over the head with it. That was Ed's punishment for smoking more than a foot away from an ashtray.

I had moved out of the hospital section on April 20, but Doc Curtin was able to keep me from going on a work detail for almost three weeks. Then it was easy work in the carpenter shop at the Kosaka Soko plant of Showa Denko, the big chemical firm. Five days later I enjoyed the heavier work of stacking heavy iron rods at the same plant, although my foot made me clumsy. I tried to be careful because Sgt. Ralph M. Knox recently had had to have a toe chopped off after an iron bar fell on his foot at the same plant. Two days later I started working with an air hammer. The bars of iron came at me on a conveyor belt—flaws had been marked by the Jap worker before me on the production line. It was my job to drill them out with the air hammer. But I had become so soft lying around the barracks that I could hardly hold the heavy hammer—let alone drill the bars. Yet by afternoon I had become fairly proficient with it, although my arms felt like lead weights. The next day, though, all this activity ended—Porky informed me that I was a diphtheria carrier and slapped me back in the hospital section. We diphtheria "bugs" were forbidden to leave the hospital section except to go to the latrine. Thankfully, the Japanese wouldn't come near us for fear of infection.

At this time, 150 prisoners from our camp moved a few miles to a camp supporting the Nippon Steel Company—some with skills had to go, and some volunteered. The volunteers wanted to get away from sadistic Japs like Shiozawa, Little Henry, and Bucktooth. Some of my friends wanted me to come after I got out of the hospital section, but I was suspicious of the rosy picture the Japs painted of conditions there—they had fooled me before at Malaybalay when I was promised a good aircraft job in Manila. We learned later that the work at Nippon Steel was harder because of the heavy steel pieces that had to be moved around.

The departing men left a lot of clothing behind with friends instead of turning it in. But the Japs had planned to collect all of this discarded clothing. When they realized what had happened, they searched everyone except the diphtheria bugs but found nothing. The men had gotten wind of the search and transferred the clothing to us in the hospital section, where it was safe because of the Japanese fear of being infected. So the shakedown was a flop, and in time everyone retrieved the clothes they had gotten from the departing prisoners.

As replacements for the 150 departing Americans, 150 native Javanese and Dutch prisoners arrived on May 22 from the populous Dutch island of Java in the East Indies. Most of the Javanese had been drafted into the Dutch Army but had been captured before finishing basic training. With the group were a few European Dutch officers.

At roll call the newcomers listed all their valuables for the Japs. More interesting to us were the quantities of salt, sugar, tea, and fine black Java pepper they had brought. Trading for these precious condiments became hot and heavy. I traded my bag of Japanese tooth powder for some pepper and salt from a Java boy who didn't realize the pepper's value here at Camp No. 2 in Kawasaki.

We diphtheria bugs had been in the hospital section for three weeks when Bucktooth Kasuya took our packs and canteens away from us. The next day he replaced our China bowls with mess kits and other canteens—this switch made no sense. Bucktooth was probably stuck with the risky job of dealing with us bugs in making these exchanges, since he was the quartermaster. But five days later, on May 30, the diphtheria scare lessened—Porky sent five of us bugs off on a work detail. Yet we did practically nothing because the Jap factory workers wouldn't come near us—having heard we were diphtheria carriers.

Warmer weather during May noticeably limited the amount of food we needed to maintain our strength. March and April had been dangerous for our health because the Japs had shut down the stoves inside on March 1 in accordance with the Emperor's decree that spring had begun. Then our chilly barracks had made us less able to keep going with the same skimpy and monotonous diet. On March 5 Porky gave the increasing number of diarrhea patients a potent shot that helped me. Porky thought another shot was necessary for us all two weeks later. On March 28 Porky tried giving diarrhea patients only soup and bread to eat, but that didn't help and didn't last. On April 7, four diarrhea patients were sent to Shinagawa Hospital. The death toll in March and April: two from malnutrition, one from dysentery, and one from beriberi.

Even after May 1 there were still beriberi patients, so Porky took them across the street and made them walk around in the dew-wet grass. But that was a one-time effort.

After the outdoor temperatures became more comfortable, countless mosquitoes swarmed into the unscreened barracks. In early July the Japs issued one mosquito net for every three men. Yet even the lucky man with a net was not well-protected at night from the little monsters. During the day they buzzed through the barracks, making random attacks. Months later, Bucktooth issued some British Army "mosquito" trousers— they reached halfway between the knees and ankles and had drawstrings.

But the next day we had to turn them in—only to get them back the following day.

Don Armstrong, the Marine with a voracious appetite, got in trouble again on June 1. This time Armstrong went into the Japs' dining area and started begging for leftovers—believing he could get away with it since the Japs sometimes did give away extra rice at the rack where they washed their bowls. But the Japs had never permitted begging. Now Armstrong had to hold an empty rice bucket at arm's length from supper time until evening roll call while missing evening chow—a worse punishment for Armstrong.

In late June I recorded a letter to my mother that was to be recorded by Radio Tokyo. To my later surprise, she got the message—it was picked up on the West Coast and sent to my mother in St. Louis.

The same day Porky encouraged one of the Javanese to get out his guitar and play some music. Soon we were singing and dancing. I was not much of a singer but joined in. All of us perked up, and three of the Japs became happily drunk with sake—Porky, Little Henry, and Lt. Saito. They were relaxed and funny as they sang songs out of tune with the already awful Japanese music coming out of the radio's loudspeaker.

The Javanese enjoyed the music and party even more than we did. However, they were sloppy soldiers and got whacked by top NCO Shiozawa for not standing at attention during roll call. When one Javanese just sat down at roll call, Shiozawa subjected him to jiu jitsu, as well as some whacks. But the Javanese didn't get angry and resentful on such occasions as Americans did—they were living better here than they did in Java.

By July 1943 I was really tired of those barracks and doing nothing—first it had taken months for my heel to mend, and then I had to stay in because I was considered to be a diphtheria carrier. I was more than ready to go out for any work and was lucky on July 4 to go on the prize detail of unloading freight at the Kawasaki railroad station. We were not closely guarded, so it was easy to steal from the food shipments—loot of the highest priority for us. While marching to the railroad station and back, I enjoyed looking around and seeing people, even though we had no way of talking to them. A few days later I worked at a coal dock—shoveling coal into piles to keep the loading platform clear.

On July 10 each of us had our picture taken to send to our nearest relative. I'm glad my mother never received it, since I had lost so much weight—my mother would not have known that I was feeling pretty good right then. Yet my short healthy period was interrupted a couple of weeks later when the factory boss sent me back to camp with ankles badly swollen from beriberi. Doc Curtin gave me a shot and then the next day insisted that I stay in—defying Sgt. Shiozawa, who scowled and shrugged his shoulders. Two days later I was back in the hospital section with swelling in the arch of my right foot. Then, during the night of July 26, I had my first attack of malaria in 1943—a night of heat and chills. The Doc gave me quinine and another beriberi shot, and in a couple of days I was back in my regular bunk.

On August 2 I was back to shoveling coal. The dust from the soft, bituminous coal settled on our face, hands, and clothes. But at the end of the day the factory boss gave a bar of soap to each five men and let us bathe in the factory bathhouse. Earlier in the month he let us

Sgt. Herbert Zincke, July 10, 1943—POW at Camp No. 2, Kawasaki; in captured British uniform for picture. (Courtesy of Herbert Zincke)

use the bathhouse, but we had no soap. At camp there had been no water two days before, and it was still scarce. Ten days later our lack of soap drove me to have a friend give me a "baldy" haircut. I figured I could keep my scalp clean with less soap. Others were doing the same thing. Bedbugs bothered us so much that summer that some of us stayed in the barracks one day to clean them out. But that effort was not completely successful. The Americans blamed the Javanese, since the bugs had not bothered us before they arrived on May 22.

Low rice rations at camp had led to a lot of pilfering at the work sites. Because of complaints from the factory boss, Shiozawa shook down all the prisoners on August 20. But we received warning soon enough not to have brought any rice back from work. As Shiozawa rummaged through our belongings, looking for rice, he ignored everything else—like back in May when he searched in vain in my bunk space for the cooked rice I was lying on and left all my belongings alone.

On August 4 I joined the mostly Javanese detail who were working at Kosaka Soko. We called it the "copper mill" because of the copperish-green, powdery chemical that was piled roof-high over a hole. Our job was to locate this hole with long poles and push the powder through the hole to a conveyor belt below. Then it was combined with ammonium nitrate to make fertilizer or explosives—we were told that fertilizer was being made. The bosses were grumpy old men who were always trying to hurry us.

The powder gave off a terrible odor, and all of us wore the gas masks the factory furnished. The Japs wore them too—the air must have been very unhealthy. The machinery was old and so noisy that my ears hurt by the end of the day. One day, at another Showa Denko plant, a conveyor belt broke and whiplashed Sgt. Reid H. Brock—causing a serious back injury.

On returning from my first day at the fertilizer factory, the cooks told us that the Japanese NCOs had helped themselves to eleven cans of our Red Cross meat and vegetable soup, plus sugar. They had probably stolen our food while drinking sake and were still drunk that night—they probably got as bored as we did. But we blamed their theft on the awful-tasting supper three days later—consisting of beans in rice and eggplant, whole fat, and tea. The next day half the camp was sick with ptomaine poisoning, so Porky put us on soup all day. I was unaffected because of my ironclad stomach.

On August 21 a new interpreter, named Kondo, arrived to replace Utsuke. We hoped for a better English speaker because it took a lot of guessing on our part to understand what Utsuke was saying. We soon were pleased on that account when Kondo questioned each one of us in good English and told us that he had spent a few years in the U.S. He had spoken to us while Porky was giving us one of his cursory physical examinations. Kondo seemed like a nice fellow, but you could never tell about Japs, from our experience so far.

In the first few weeks we liked being able to understand Kondo, but on September 14 he and Lt. Saito got drunk together after evening roll call. They called us back into formation and had us count off repeatedly—just for laughs. We were finally dismissed at 8:30 P.M. But a few days later Kondo noticed Oliver Gilbert, a chow hound, about to be beaten by a guard. Gilbert looked like he was about to beg for leftovers from Japs before they washed their food trays. Kondo had enough clout to call off the guard, since Gilbert hadn't actually begged. As time went on, Kondo liked to talk to us one-on-one when no guard could hear. I found him to be a good listener, and he had interesting things to say. When I predicted that the U.S. would win the war, there were no blows, just disagreement.

A few days later, Gilbert could not be saved. He was sitting down and did not get up and bow when the camp commander, Lt. Saito, passed by;

as an officer and camp commander, Saito had god-like power over every-one—Shiozawa, the other NCOs, guards, and us. Saito usually had Shiozawa handle discipline and punishment, but Saito himself beat up Gilbert this time. Gilbert had been beaten by Shiozawa the month before because he was not standing at attention at roll call. But he kept on break-ing rules and trying to make friends with the NCOs and guards. In con-trast, I always tried to be as unnoticeable as possible.

Later in September Lt. Saito struck again. It started at another shake-down—we didn't know what they were looking for. But Moore and Pfc. Grant Kendrick were the culprits. Both Saito and Shiozawa beat them up; Saito knocked Kendrick down and kicked him—breaking two ribs. Two nights later Saito threw a party in the Japanese meeting room. The Javanese musicians entertained the Japanese staff and office girls while Saito got drunk again. The Japs were having drinking parties every night that kept going after lights were out. Usually I could go right to sleep more readily than most, but they kept even me awake for a long time on September 29.

The muscular Shiozawa had found many victims among us for him and his guards to beat ever since our arrival last November. When he couldn't find a rule infraction, he created one. Earlier in the year he trapped my friend Lubiewski by giving him a cigarette to smoke where smoking was forbidden—a beating followed. In late August Shiozawa had whacked Pfc. Arnold for bringing an onion into the barracks. Sgt. Wyllsey got the same punishment for letting Arnold do it—Wyllsey was supposed to keep the barracks clean.

Yet Shiozawa suffered a kind of payback about this time. Doc Curtin confided to a few of us that Shiozawa had come to him with syphilis. Dur-ing the painful treatment, Doc told us, "I was happy for the chance to make him suffer in the painful procedure that was necessary." Doc recalled being swatted when he had vigorously objected after Shiozawa insisted on send-ing sick men out to work.

After Doc Curtin treated him, Shiozawa was sent to Shinagawa Hos-pital. We were glad to have him gone and then surprised to hear some giggling from the guards' barracks the first night after Shiozawa had left. We soon realized that the guards had invited some girls to visit them—something that Shiozawa would never permit. But the party didn't seem to bother Lt. Saito, the camp commander, because we heard giggles for several more nights until Shiozawa returned in a week, fit as ever.

XI

My Friendly Factory Boss

September 16, 1943, to December 31, 1943

In the middle of September, Sgt. W. R. Stewart, Moore, and I were unloading nitric acid from tank cars when those two spilled some acid and badly burned their legs. Then a friendly-looking 60-year-old civilian came over to see what had happened. After the men had been taken care of, the old man turned to chat with me. We communicated pretty well with my smattering of Japanese and sign language. He was the boss of a work detail at another plant and was having trouble getting his Javanese workers to understand what he wanted them to do. When he found out I was a staff sergeant, he immediately asked me if I wanted to take charge of the Javanese. I asked him about the noise doing his work because of the severe ear problems I was having at the copper mill. He assured me there would be no excessive noise. I acted pleased by all this attention, even though I didn't know what I was getting into. But I had no say. I doubted how much authority he had anyway, so I doubted anything would happen.

But back at camp a few days later on September 22, Sgt. Shiozawa gave me a form to sign that requested permanent assignment to the friendly old man's work detail. The next day I marched a dozen or so Americans out to the new work site. There was the old man—all smiles now that he had gotten me to manage his work. He told me what he wanted done for the day and walked off—leaving me with my Americans and about the same number of Javanese, who had already arrived from our camp. I mingled the Javanese with Americans so there would be no excuse for them not to know what to do. If the men finished before the end of the day, they could come back and just relax. Apparently the old man was responsible for taking items needed for manufacturing out of storage, as well as keeping a number of buildings cleaned up. While walking around to see how everyone was doing, I noticed some loose clothing and soap lying around. A light went on in my head—my detail could use these items for themselves or for trading. By early afternoon my men had finished all the jobs and were just sitting around when the old boss returned. After he looked around and saw that everything was done, he invited us into the rest shack.

Inside on a large table stood a teapot, cookies, and mugs. We were soon sitting around on benches, enjoying the snack. The old man sat down beside me and let me know—mostly by gesture—how satisfied he was with the work that had been done. He called me by my latest POW designation, #18. Another day I discovered the old man's name while he was bragging about #18's work to another boss. Then when I addressed the old man by name, he asked me mine. Thereafter we were on a name basis—unlike the barracks where the guards knew us only by our numbers.

During our second day with the old man, he walked away again on his own business. After apportioning the work among my crew, I told them to pick up anything of value that could be carried in their clothes. At the end of the day the Javanese were more successful than the Americans. They came back with their clothes bulging and tossed the loot into an empty storage bin the factory was not using. They explained that they had already worked out a trading scheme with the Koreans. An hour later, before we went back to camp, a couple of grinning Koreans came back from the storage bin with bulges around their waists. They had taken what they wanted and left cigarettes for us—cigarettes were their specialty. The Americans also became adept at thievery, so my American-Javanese work detail carried on continuous trading with the Koreans working for Showa Denko— Japanese industry had been using conscripted Korean labor since 1938.*

I believe the boss knew that our stealing and trading was going on. His 18 to 20-year-old assistant Guchi, who sometimes followed me around, did not object when I told one of the men about an item he should pick up. Guchi did not seem to be keeping track of me—he may have been in training to be a boss. One day when I suffered cramps, Guchi took me into the rest shack and gave me tea and six pills. But I was still in poor shape by the end of the day, so the next ranking NCO on my detail marched the men back to camp.

---

*Such conscription was forbidden by the International Labor Organization Convention, which Japan signed in 1930 and ratified in 1932. Holmes, Unjust Enrichment, page 21.

On the morning of October 5 the camp guards had us stand naked before our bunks and rub ourselves down with towels for ten minutes— supposedly a health and fitness measure. They told us this was to be a daily thing, but I hoped it wouldn't go into winter. The next day a more serious matter arose—the guards kept us in formation after evening roll call to watch the chow hound Armstrong be severely beaten for supposedly stealing bread, meat, and sugar the night before.

We had been appalled by Armstrong's punishment on March 13 for the same thing—Doc Curtin tried to save him from probable permanent damage. Now, we didn't believe Armstrong was the culprit. There was still more trouble for Armstrong the next day because Armstrong's factory boss told Shiozawa that Armstrong was suspected of taking something from the factory. Of course, Shiozawa had a shakedown to find whatever it was. Tension stayed high the next day because we thought Armstrong's treatment was unjust.

At 10:30 P.M. Shiozawa took everyone who slept near Armstrong to Lt. Saito's office. There Saito, the interpreter Kondo, Bucktooth Kasuya, and Porky Watanabe were waiting for us. Since I slept nearest Armstrong, I was the first to be questioned. Saito began by asking me if Armstrong was guilty. I was so worried about Armstrong after his earlier savage punishment that I blurted out, "I don't believe Armstrong did it." Saito didn't need Kondo to translate for him—he scowled and pulled out his samurai sword. I was terrified as he lifted the sword above my head and brought it down. The next thing I knew, I was on my knees. Then I realized why I was alive. Saito had hit me with the flat of his sword.

Saito's blow to me discouraged any more of the group from speaking up for Armstrong when they were questioned. But Saito was still angry, so he had us stand at attention for an hour. Then we all gave in to the extent of saying that "Armstrong seemed to be guilty." But that wasn't enough for Saito; he had Shiozawa muster the whole camp at 12:30 A.M. and kept us at attention while all section heads reported to Saito's office and declared Armstrong was guilty. We got to bed at 2:00 A.M.

I did not always get to work at my friendly boss's work site. In the afternoon of October 15 I began unloading nitric acid from tank cars at another part of the Showa Denko complex. Guchi had come over from my normal work site to see me—the young man seemed to work or not, and roam as he pleased. As he watched, I attached the pump to the tank car that was to lift the nitric acid to a reservoir, which lay above the track. But when I activated the pump, nitric acid splattered all over the lower part of my body—a gasket must have loosened or worn out. Without conscious thought, I leaped into a ditch full of dirty water along the track and sank to my waist in it.

Guchi was unhurt and called the local boss, a doctor, and the security guards. Other sympathetic onlookers soon surrounded me. The factory doctor put some salve on my legs before I was carried back to the barracks on a stretcher.

The next day Doc Curtin kept me in and put more salve on. The following day the Doc reluctantly let me go out to stack lumber—Porky thought I could do that job. But by 3 P.M. I had to quit because my knees hurt so much. They took me over to the doctor who had first looked at my burns; since I was to be working there every day, he could treat and bandage my legs as necessary. But that lasted only a few days because my knees were becoming infected. On October 19 Doc Curtin took over and kept me in the barracks. The next day Doc put me in the hospital section. Being inside, I felt colder in the late October weather than when working outside. But at least in the hospital section you could avoid the naked rubdown every morning that was required in the healthy section.

Lt. Saito caught a Javanese who had sneaked into the latrine to avoid the rubdown. After dismissing the Americans, Saito kept the Javanese lined up for some time—but not at attention, as would have been the case in punishing Americans. We believed the Japs went easy on the Javanese since they were fellow Asians and thus members of the Japs' Co-Prosperity Zone.

In late October the acid burns on my legs had healed enough for me to go out and work, but then my heel acted up again, so Doc Curtin opened and drained it. The next day Curtin ordered me to stay in. I was reluctant because of the chilly barracks, but kept warm by helping Sgt. C. L. Richards build a good fire in the bathhouse. The Japs allowed hot baths in the cooler weather, even though no stoves could be lit in the barracks until January 1—winter's beginning, according to the Emperor.

Kondo recognized the cooler weather by informing us, "You can all let your hair grow long and grow beards to keep warmer now that it's getting cold out." We could barely hold back our laughter until Kondo was out of hearing. Later that day at evening roll call, Kondo announced that everyone was to buy a notebook and start a diary. But, against regulations, I had already been keeping two diaries: one that was non-critical of the Japs that I kept in my bunking space, and another—the real one—which I carried in my shirt pocket. The Kempetai, the Japanese secret police, had already found my innocuous diary—but they gave it back to me and told me to continue it. Instead of diaries being forbidden, we were now ordered to keep them.

In early November I spent most of two miserable days re-threading rusty bolts with a tap and die while exposed to the cold and rain. One of the afternoons when I changed to unloading nitric acid cars, my young friend Guchi came by to give me a cigarette holder made of bamboo. I liked him, but we had a hard time talking because my Japanese was not so good, and neither was his English.

On November 11 I had my first uninterrupted night's sleep in a year—it was wonderful! I had been getting up before midnight and once later because of so much water in my system. In January and February, when the barracks were heated, it was cold in the latrine, which was never heated. All of us suffered in the same way because of our diet. Last night was good for us because we had a loaf of bread and fried fish for supper. We had had better food the last few months, but not in enough quantity to keep us from losing more weight—I reached a low of 125 pounds on November 20.

November 12 was the one-year anniversary at the Mitsui Madhouse. There were no work details in the afternoon, and at 3 P.M. we had a snack of burnt rice. Then Kondo told us we all had to shave—so much for the idea of growing beards to keep warm. We soon found the reason for shaving. Shiozawa assembled us across the street for group pictures. The guards wanted to be in the pictures too, so they were. Then we had hot baths in the bathhouse and a supper of sweet spuds, sweetened beans, a stew of meat, onion, and cabbage, and tea. After dinner the Javanese sang for us, and finally we Americans put our hearts into singing the "Star-Spangled Banner."

When I worked with the tank cars, Guchi was always there—maybe he was worried I would get burned with acid again. The day after the celebration Guchi again was there, making my work on a cold day pleasant. Four days later I was at the same work site—this time repairing broken acid lines. I couldn't understand how any of their machinery and equipment would work because everything was in need of repair or replacement. These Japs certainly did more with less than we would have expected. Could that be why we were POWs?

In late November the guards caught a Javanese stealing something, but Shiozawa didn't do anything about it. The Javanese were getting away with murder compared to us Americans. This was another instance of the guards going easy on the Javanese since they were fellow Asians who were to benefit from the Co-Prosperity Zone.

Opposite: Group of POWs and Japanese guards, November 12, 1943—the first anniversary of our imprisonment at Camp No. 2, Kawasaki. Identified by number are: 1. PFC Jackfert, 2. PFC Armstrong, 3. F/1 Mailloux, Navy, 4. Sgt. Britton, 5. PFC Nuzzo, medic, 6. PFC Lubiewski, 7. Sgt. Hoy, 8. Sgt. Zincke, 9. Lt. Saito. (Photograph supplied by the author)

That same day I worked under a different boss at Showa Denko—pouring lead into ingots. I was slow at this heavy work. When the boss tried to hurry me up, I cussed him out. Then he whacked me over the head with a wooden shoe. I guess I asked for it, but I was mad enough to kill him. Then I was afraid that Shiozawa would find out. But nothing happened back at camp. Had Guchi talked this boss out of reporting me? In any case, I was back with Guchi and my favorite boss on December 2. After my crew stacked bricks all day, the friendly boss gave us some sweet spuds.

Food continued to be better in December, and my body showed it. My weight had gone up to 133 pounds—from 125 a month before. My chest measured 35 inches and waist 30 inches—pretty good compared to the other Americans.

The next day eight letters really cheered me up—one from my sister-in-law, one from my girlfriend, and, best of all, six letters from my stepmother. She was more than anyone could wish for in a mother.

The following day the food situation continued to improve—one American Red Cross parcel for each man, plus something from British Red Cross packages. The next day we celebrated Christmas with group pictures and church services, conducted by Commander Loojen, the Dutch submarine skipper—we had no chaplains. Again there was lots of food. Then on December 30 a box from my stepmother brought still more food. I wolfed down the box of raisins she sent and paid for it with diarrhea for three days.

Opposite: Another group of POWs and Japanese guards, November 12, 1943—the first anniversary of our imprisonment at Camp No. 2, Kawasaki. Identified by number are: 1. Lt. Cmdr. Loojen, 2. Lt. Carney, 3. 1st Sgt. Shiozawa, 4. Lt. Myazaki, 5. Cpl. Watanabe, 6. Sgt. McCool, 7. Sgt.Wyllsey, 8. Sgt. "Blackie" Young, 9. Sgt. Richards, 10. Pvt. Hough, 11. Sgt. Kasuya, 12. Lt. Curtin, British doctor. (Photograph supplied by the author)

XII

Never Enough to Eat

January 1, 1944, to October 31, 1944

On New Year's Day of 1944, 90 prisoners at Camp No. 2 went off to work, but 200 of us celebrated with no work and a cookie apiece—a treat from the POW officers, who were paid but didn't have to work.

On January 3 Doc Curtin moved me back to the hospital section, where I had spent so much time in the first part of 1943. Now my heel had become infected again. Lack of enough good food lessened my body's resistance. But since I couldn't go to work, my ration was cut in half, so I had still less strength to fight off the infection. One good thing, though, the whole barracks was kept warm now because the stoves were lit because winter started on January 1, according to the Emperor's calendar. After five days I was still in the hospital section. Doc Curtin peeled off lots of dead skin from my heel, but a sore had developed on my left calf.

The Doc, always neatly dressed in his British uniform, was having his own trouble. Bucktooth Kasuya, the quartermaster, had recently slapped the doctor and Private Grant Warner for unknown reasons. Sgt. Shiozawa, the top noncom, usually whacked us or had the guards do it. About this time, Shiozawa enjoyed slapping some men for not having their blouses buttoned up at roll call.

January 19 was a bad night for me because I had to make so many trips to the latrine—we had had beans with barley for supper. My weight then was down to 127 pounds from 133 the month before—the result of the reduced rations that came when I did not work.

Three days later I moved out of the hospital section but didn't go out on detail. But when I tried to work on February 4, my heel gave me so much pain that I went back to the hospital section that evening—again facing half-rations. I sweated it out the next day when Porky and an outside inspection team selected me for removal to Shinagawa Hospital. Doc Curtin had saved me from going there in early 1943 because he believed the hospital would simply amputate my foot because of my infected heel. Now in 1944 the Jap inspectors were trying to move me again, but Doc stuck out his neck and kept me under his care. That hospital was successful in other types of cases for some of us, but a Javanese had recently died of pneumonia there.

On February 10 I received six letters from my mother and one from a girl in East St. Louis, whom I didn't know. We closely studied her long-winded letter because of its war news. It was carefully worded to get by Japanese censors but revealed American successes in New Guinea and Alaska amid flowery praise for Japanese astuteness. It called Japanese retreats victories and must have befuddled the censors. But it was a great boost to our morale—we had had no reliable news of the war since our surrender in the spring of 1942. The letter was dated August 20, 1943, and the writer's name was Isabel Dotterman. The return address was simply East St. Louis, and I was never able to locate her after the war.

By February 23 I was hungrier than ever because I was still in the hospital section on half-rations. So I was eager to rejoin the rice conspiracy when Blackie Young asked me. He and C. L. Richards, also a crane operator, were still cooking rice on their crane and still needed a good place in the hospital section to store the cooked rice until it could be distributed. The day after I joined, February 24, was my 25th birthday. Blackie and Richards gave me a most appropriate gift—a large plate of white rice equal to two times our usual ration. I had to save some of it for the next day. I had been on hospital rations from January 2 to March 1, but the rice conspiracy succeeded in bringing my weight up to 146 pounds on April 20—I had reached a low of 122 pounds on January 3. My hunger had overcome the fear of getting caught after I had quit the rice conspiracy the year before when Sgt. Shiozawa had climbed into my bunk space to search my belongings while I lay on top of some rice Blackie had delivered.

We cleaned and sprayed the barracks on May 2—hoping to get rid of the fleas. The same day, the Americans moved to the second floor and the Javanese moved to the first floor. The Javanese were so messy and flea-infested that the guards, as well as the Americans, wanted to keep all the Javanese together. Yet the flea problem persisted. On July 4 the fleas kept me up all night, and on July 11 we spent all morning trying to get rid of the fleas that the Javanese had left behind on the second floor.

About this time, Kondo, the interpreter, offered to give Japanese language instruction to one or two of us in each section—we were organized in sections of 12 or more for chow rations. But even though Kondo was easy to get along with—I enjoyed talking with him—he had no takers for his language classes. Yet many of us did our best to pick up Japanese on our own. I often jotted down new words that I heard so I could find out their meaning later from an American or my favorite factory boss at Showa Denko.

On June 7, 1944, the guards ordered us to goose-step in and out of the camp gate as we marched to work and returned—a crazy way to copy the Japs' ally, Nazi Germany, because German soldiers, not their prisoners, were the goose-steppers. At Kawasaki Camp No. 2 we succeeded in looking so ridiculous that the Japs lost face and went back to the simple hand salute as we marched out and back through the gate. Sgt. Shiozawa didn't stay angry about this. When he inspected my bowl bag and bedding a couple of days later, he wasn't satisfied, and drew a fish on my pillow slip and joked, "Fish needs water." I wisely did some more washing.

Because of the heat in June and lack of soap, I had my friend Richards shave my head to keep my scalp clean. In addition, after July 1, shortage of water made it still more difficult to keep clean. By July 17 there was no water, but it soon became available in small quantities but was short for the rest of the summer.

On August 1 we formed on the vacant lot across the street for Lt. Saito, the camp commander, to recognize the prisoners with the most working days and highest efficiency rating. Their reward was a cup of tea or grape juice, plus cigarettes. I had been in the hospital too long to be considered, but wouldn't have minded being left out. From 1 to 3 P.M., Javanese guitarists and singers performed for Lt. Saito, three girls from the Mitsui corporate offices, and us. Then everyone got a snack of sweetened beans and a small dumpling.

By August 6 I was feeling so good I volunteered to unload coal. I was getting bored with working at Showa Denko, even when I worked with the friendly old boss. Another consideration was the large, half-coolie lunch we got on the coal-unloading detail. That day fifty men were sent back to camp at noon because they were needed for unloading that night—there was always a sense of urgency about unloading the coal ships because of the success of American submarines in attacking Japanese shipping, we believed. My group returned to camp at 4 P.M. To cap off a busy day's work, we had to stand at attention from 8 to 10 P.M. because of sloppy counting-off at roll call.

A couple of weeks later, however, I was glad to be on work detail

USS *Narwhal*—one of the U.S. submarines that played havoc with Japanese shipping. (U.S. Naval Historical Center)

with the friendly old boss. I had wrenched my back while moving a 350-pound cylinder of ammonia. Doc Curtin did his best with salve and taping, but I could do little work the next day. The following day the old boss let me take it easy in the rest shack. The next day, though, the old boss thought I was gold-bricking so put me back to work—the only time he had questioned my willingness to work. A week later I took the bandage off my back because of the heat, but my back was no better. Now the old boss was convinced my back problem was real. He insisted that I do no work myself but just see that the rest of the detail got the work done.

One day in early September we had a wonderful day at Showa Denko—the old boss didn't show up and it rained all day. I had us all stay in the rest shack—I would have been mobbed if I tried to get them to work unless we had to. The roving guard from camp didn't care because the Japanese Army got paid for us to show up—whether we worked or not.

But trouble was brewing at camp the same day—about a Javanese who had lost his work jacket. The guards thought it had been stolen but couldn't find it in the morning shakedown. The next day the Javanese prisoners did not come back to camp at the regular time. We finally heard them come in at 4 A.M. Then Shiozawa made them all sit at attention in the mess hall while Watanabe and Shiozawa beat the hell out of the Javanese who had stolen the jacket. Finally, Shiozawa had the groggy thief beaten some more by the man who had lost the jacket—the guards looked on to make sure the additional beating was severe enough.

I deserted the old boss again on September 10 when I learned of a detail that earned you an extra ration of rice. That, plus being bored again, persuaded me to spend the day unloading sacks of fertilizer from six box cars and loading one car. But the next day the old boss growled at me for going on another detail, and I was in his doghouse for a few days.

By September 21 I was so bored with getting the men to do simple tasks on the old man's detail that I traded with someone to go back to unloading coal. We stood in the hold shoveling coal onto cargo nets that were lifted out of the ship by Blackie Young or Richards, our POW crane operators (they also ran the rice conspiracy). But the shoveling job was not good—when the cargo nets were lifted, they dropped smaller chunks of coal among us, and the masks we always wore on work details were of little use in the foul air in the ships' dark holds. The muscle-bound coolies who worked among us jeered at our feeble shoveling efforts. Yet I liked it as a change, and especially liked the extra half-coolie ration of food.

But I was worried when Master Sgt. John W. Britton told me he was permanently assigning me to coal-unloading since I had been trading details so much. Britton and M/Sgt. Wyllsey were the top-ranking non-coms among the American prisoners. Britton had taken responsibility for the daily assignment of the camp's work details. Taller than I, Britton was nearing 50 and had worked himself up in the Army Air Corps to Master Sergeant. Before surrendering, he had been Flight Line Chief for maintenance of aircraft in combat. That experience made him comfortable with his POW job.

Yet we did not resent his working with the Japs because at times he was able to use his position to shield American prisoners from the guards. At other times such efforts failed. One time Britton noticed Private Gilbert, a notorious chow hound, begging leftovers from the Japs at the wash basin where they washed their food trays. One of the guards was about to pounce on Gilbert for this flagrant violation of camp rules against begging.

But Britton got to Gilbert first and ordered, "Get back to your bunk, Gilbert, and stay there." Turning to the guard, Britton declared, "Gilbert will pay for this." The guard just shrugged, not wanting to buck the ranking American non-com who had responsibility for organizing the camp's labor details.

Now I had complicated Britton's job of filling out daily work details by trading jobs with men in other details without letting him know. But the Japs were calling the shots, because the next day a guard sent me back to the old man's work detail despite Britton's wanting to keep me at unloading coal.

Yet on October 5 I was unloading coal again—a task so urgent that we had to stay until we were finished. We were still working at 4 P.M. but broke for a whole coolie lunch, and then at 11 P.M. we got a camp ration plus a half-coolie ration. Later, a guard caught me prowling around the ship in the dark—I was just looking around out of curiosity. He gave me a good slap and sent me back to work. I figured that nothing more would come of it after I was given a whole coolie ration when we completed unloading at 2:30 A.M.

But back on another urgent unloading job eight days later I paid for my earlier wandering around the ship by not getting the standard half-coolie lunch at noon. At 4 P.M., however, I got my full coolie ration. Yet we had been back at work for only ten minutes when Blackie Young's winch broke down—he could no longer lift the cargo nets out of the hold, so we went back to camp full of food without doing the work that was supposed to go with it.

We believed the hurry-up unloading of the coal ships resulted from fear of attacks by American submarines or coal shortages caused by previous sinkings. Postwar analysis shows that the problem of faulty American torpedoes had not been corrected until 1943—probably saving my life, because the torpedo fired at our prison ship by an American submarine on October 9, 1942, broke water and missed.

With the use of effective torpedoes in 1944, however, American submarines sank 600 Japanese ships, or 2.7 million tons, as compared to 2.2 million tons sunk in 1941, 1942, and 1943 combined. But submariners paid heavily—22 percent of American submarines failed to return from combat patrols, resulting in the highest casualty rate of any branch of service.*

The Japs gave us the day off after we unloaded coal until 2:30 A.M. on October 6. I got up in the afternoon and went downstairs to chat with some of the Javanese who knew enough English for some conversation. They were pretty nice fellows, who were probably living better here than at home. But we were in the same boat—color and nationality made no difference. Who am I to judge who is better, anyway?

Lt. Saito and Bucktooth Kasuya left camp on October 12—good riddances. But Saito was back twelve days later and decided the barracks area of my chow section was not clean enough. Shiozawa had me sweep it up.

On October 27 I was back at Showa Denko on an easy job with the old boss. It was raining, but we didn't suffer because he gave us indoor jobs. Even though he didn't like my going off and unloading coal, he put up with me and kept us all dry. I liked the old guy.

On October 31 I joined the team of 100 men who were to unload a

Ronald H. Spector, Eagle Against the Sun *(Free Press, 1985), pages 486–87.*

coal ship. But I had an easy day because there were too many of us to use effectively. I had time to observe the muscular coolies working, jabbering to themselves, and throwing lumps of coal at us to get us to work harder. Yet the ship wasn't organized to use us after 2 P.M., so we sat in the mess hall until returning to camp. That night we had a very tasty meal of rice and batter-fried sweet potatoes, but it was not really enough to satisfy a hungry soldier.

XIII

Early B-29 Raids

November 1, 1944, to January 17, 1945

The Japanese had not been able to make effective use of the surplus POW manpower they had on October 31 to complete the urgent unloading of a coal ship. My day crew had to work on the job the next day. The night crew had left us with small, dusty chunks of coal to shovel off the deck onto the cargo net. Then when Blackie, our POW crane operator, lifted the net, we were showered with coal dust and small pieces of coal. At noon they rewarded us with a full coolie lunch and one cigarette.

At 1:45 P.M. we were back at work when one of us looked out of the hold and saw vapor trails high in the sky. Sure enough, contrails were tailing out of a single four-engined aircraft that was flying so high that AA fire from nearby ships fell far short. The ships around us sounded their sirens. On our ship the coolies clambered out of the hold and squelched our shouts of joy by slamming down the hatches. But our camp guard made them let us out and double-timed us back to camp.

After the war we learned that we had seen the first B-29 over Tokyo — it was called a Superfortress and was about three times larger than the B-17 Flying Fortress. On this day, flying at 32,000 feet, the B-29 crew could see the streets of Tokyo surging with activity. For thirty-five minutes the B-29 stayed over the west side of Tokyo Bay while the photo-navigator trained his cameras on the factories crowded along the shore from Tokyo to Yokohama. Enemy fighters were airborne, but apparently did not want to attack at that altitude.*

*Steve Birdsall, Saga of the Superfortress (Doubleday, 1980), page 110.

Formation of B-29s ("Superfortresses") over Mt. Fujiyama—the first B-29 high over Kawasaki cheered the POWs and dampened the morale of the guards. (National Archives, 342-FH-3B25882-63370)

At our camp near the shore in Kawasaki, all the work details were back by 2:45 P.M. Everyone had a smile on his face as we patted each other on the back and said it wouldn't be long until we got out of there. But Kondo, the interpreter, explained in his garbled English that we had seen the highest-flying Japanese aircraft, which was on a reconnaissance mission. We burst out laughing at Kondo's remarkable explanation. He just grinned and walked away.

The sight of the B-29 caused our morale to surge—we could take anything after seeing this example of American military might. We reasoned that the boys in that B-29 had been able to take excellent pictures of Tokyo and Yokohama because of the clear day.

The next day the coolies on the same ship—which still had not been unloaded—no longer jeered at us but were strangely quiet. They looked at us with an expression that almost showed respect. I worked in a hold where they had a lot of trouble with the winches, so we didn't have much shoveling to do. But we got a half-coolie lunch and one cigarette anyway. In the afternoon Richards gave me a half-ration of rice for doing his sweeping in the barracks—I was always looking for ways to satisfy my hunger.

Air raid sirens stopped unloading at 10:30 A.M. on November 5, and the All Clear signal sounded at noon. Even after that break I did as little as possible because I was stiff and sore from shoveling coal the past few days.

The next day the galley received a 274-pound pig—supposedly to be part of the feast planned for November 12 to celebrate our two-year anniversary at Camp No. 2, Kawasaki. But when we noticed Lt. Saito and Kondo watching the pig being butchered, we were not surprised that many pork chops disappeared from the galley.

When the big day arrived, we were off work, had plenty to eat, and enjoyed singing, music and dancing by the Javanese. But the only sign of the pig was a cup of pork onion soup. Most of the pork was probably consumed at a loud Japanese party the night before.

Even though it became very cold the night of November 13, Sgt. Mizuno would not let us wear overcoats the next day—like not using the heating stoves in the barracks, wearing overcoats was not permitted until January 1. But unloading sacks of cement kept our detail warm. When we stopped in mid-afternoon, we looked like ghosts because of the cement dust. But we washed ourselves at the factory bathhouse before returning to camp.

A few days later I enjoyed a day on the old boss's detail. He was so glad to see me that he let me stay in the rest shack all day. I tended the fire while my crew did the outside work on a cold day; but I got sick from the rotten sweet potatoes we had for lunch, so I had to go on sick call after supper. Then I craved a cigarette so much that I carried Murdock's chow buckets for one cigarette, even though I thought I had broken the habit a few weeks before.

A few days after our second anniversary at Camp No. 2, a dozen Americans and a few Javanese, visiting from downstairs, asked me to sing some songs with them. I had no talent but was glad enough to join in. The two groups had gotten together after the Javanese had asked the Americans if they were interested in music. We sang several times with the help of a Javanese guitar, but we never put on a show.

On November 24 air-raid sirens sent us into a large tunnel at 12:30 P.M. We were there until 2 P.M. and then marched back to camp, where we found that a gas tank nearby had accidentally caught fire. Worried that it might spread, we began to load our personal gear on hand carts so we would be ready to evacuate. While we stood by in a state of uncertainty, a group of B-29s flew very high above us, heading southward from Tokyo toward Yokohama.

We thought they were taking photos of the large industrial area between the two cities. Nearby ships and shore guns fired, but the bursts were way too low and well behind the bombers, which were moving faster than the AA gunners realized. Nor could the Japanese pursuit planes get high enough to challenge the B-29s. But I learned after the war that this was not a photo mission. The B-29s caused some fires in Tokyo—the next day the *New York Daily News* reported Tokyo to be "ablaze after the raid." Yet the destruction in Tokyo that day was mild compared to the destruction it would suffer in 1945.

At Camp No. 2 our men soon brought the fire under control. All Clear was sounded at 3:30 P.M., so we took our gear back into the barracks. Then a complete blackout was ordered before dark but was soon canceled. Two days later a single B-29 flew over in the early afternoon. The next day, when three blasts—meaning a local alert—sounded at noon, we were sent back to camp. We crowded into the downstairs of the barracks and were told to sit on the floor with overcoats and blankets over our heads. We were huddled in the Javanese sleeping area, but they had not been recalled from work. I came to notice that they were never recalled—after the war it was learned that white prisoners were considered of greater value by Japanese factories.*

There was no air raid on November 28. That night Lt. Saito, Sgt. Shiozawa, and Sgt. Mizuno got drunk and took roll call without lining us up.

During the first November 30 alert, we Americans carried our bedding downstairs for crowded sleeping with the Javanese. All Clear sent us back upstairs, but the cycle was repeated before the night was over. The second time downstairs we didn't sleep much because AA guns were firing from the roof of a nearby building, and a Japanese pursuit plane was flying around.

At evening roll call on December 1, Navy Lt. Carney relayed instructions to have our clothes ready for moving at a moment's notice—we had already done that. But we should not worry because we were told the Japanese had taken measures to protect us. Camp routine would continue as usual, plus there would now be calisthenics daily. But I had been getting plenty of exercise the past few days unloading cement and medical equipment from freight cars. The calisthenics did not materialize.

There were no raids on December 2, and the weather was beautiful. Yet the old boss kept me in the rest shack tending the fire and

---

*As early as September 1942, Japanese industry urgently requested white labor from military prison camps. Mitsui, Mitsubishi, and Kawasaki Heavy Industries provided their own ships to transport the POWs to Japan and elsewhere. Holmes, Unjust Enrichment, pages 22–23.

making tea. I was thinking he hoped for some of my Red Cross parcel at Christmas.

December 7 started with a siren at 4:15 A.M. Then during the day we had an earthquake that lasted only one minute and did no damage. Finally, sirens blew at evening chow, and a short blackout followed.

A general alarm on December 10 was followed by three blasts. This was the signal for a local raid, so we had an immediate blackout. Later we saw searchlights and AA firing over Tokyo, and heard bombs exploding. AA firing from the nearby power plant woke us up that night. But we went back to sleep before All Clear.

I had dropped a heavy sheet of copper on my finger on November 30. Ichtheol salve had not helped, so Doc Curtin cut it open on December 16. Yet I felt nothing because of two numbing shots at the base of my finger. Wonderful! But two days later my finger hurt like hell when Doc cleaned it. The old boss was not sympathetic—he just told me to go out and work with the rest of the men. I didn't mind because I had felt guilty staying in the rest shack in recent days.

December 19 was different because for once the Americans got off easier than the Javanese. That day Shiozawa and his new assistant, Kittani, shook down the whole camp—the factories had complained about pilfering by the POWs. The guards found much loot among the Javanese— coconut oil, fish oil, rice, bean powder, and clothing. But little was found among the Americans, who are not so adept or as eager to loot, so we escaped punishment. Shiozawa had the guards beat hell out of the guilty Javanese, and confiscated the stolen goods. The Javanese in my singing group escaped punishment, so we sang in the bathhouse. I did it mainly just to break the monotony.

On December 21 Lt. Saito, the camp commander, found Gilbert using the latrine before roll call and beat him very badly. Gilbert frequently got in trouble with the guards for stealing food and breaking rules, but Saito had no good reason for going after him this time. Saito's apparent pretext was the restriction on using the bathhouse before evening roll call, but Gilbert had not gone near the bathhouse. Chorus practice again—I must have been really bored to keep on with it.

We started celebrating Christmas the night before with carols and a whole Red Cross parcel for each of us. The section leaders reported all present at 8 P.M., but Shiozawa conducted no roll call and let us keep lights on until 10 P.M. A general Alarm interrupted sleep at 2:30 A.M.

I started on my food parcel at 7:30 A.M. Christmas morning by fixing myself a cup of coffee with milk and sugar, which I drank with sweet potatoes and a half can of butter. By 9 A.M. I had also eaten two chocolate bars, a pound of butter, a box of raisins, and a can of powdered milk. I felt wonderful! For lunch I had a loaf of bread, a cup of thick curried beef, potatoes, and lettuce stew. But that afternoon I couldn't make it to the singing and dancing program downstairs. I was so gassed up from the rich food I had eaten so hoggishly that I had to hit the sack. But I felt better by supper and enjoyed eating some more.

The day after Christmas I was back at work with the old boss. Hoping to satisfy his hopes for something good from my Red Cross parcel, I fixed him a cup of stateside coffee with cream in it. But he took a taste and barked, "No good!" I hadn't put any sugar in it. I could have wrung his damn neck right on the spot! He is nuts if he thinks I'm going to give him any of my precious sugar! I had a good day, however, despite the old man's complaint. Back at camp, Kondo, the interpreter, told us we would get another Red Cross food parcel if the inspection the day after tomorrow went off OK.

The inspection finally came on December 28. Lt. Saito and his boys inspected the camp and then went out to the work sites to check on us there. Everything must have been all right because no one got the hell beaten out of him. They had finished before another alert sounded in mid-afternoon. Still no food parcels, but there were favorable rumors. That night we had another earthquake and three air-raid alerts. My weight had moved up to 145 pounds—my Christmas eating orgy must have had some effect.

On the last day of the year there was a large coal-unloading detail that I wanted to join, but I had to go on an easier detail because my finger had not healed completely. When the work details came back, Kondo shook us down, looking for Red Cross food taken out on the job. Luckily, he found nothing because we had eaten it all. After supper, Kondo gave us the long-hoped-for Red Cross food parcels

Nineteen forty-five began with more of the same—four alerts the night before New Year's Day and then a good work day with the old boss, who gave each of us two tangerines. As the Emperor decreed, stoves were lit on January 1, so the barracks became comfortable (and a little snow on January 6 did not bother us).

But the day of the snow I discovered some damn crabs on me. I had no alternative but to shave clean, since there was no soap available—it was rough! I was able to take a hot bat after unloading coal until 10 P.M. Back at camp the Doc gave me some salve to make sure the crabs were dead. I hit the sack immediately, but the fire guard shook me at midnight since I was scheduled to relieve him. Incredibly, I had arranged to stand a second hour of fire watch to pay back Murdock for a rice ration, so I didn't hit the sack again until 2 A.M.

The next day I enjoyed talking about the outcome of the war with the old boss and his assistant, "Fangs." Fangs was a little, stubby guy with only two teeth in his head—his two canine teeth. Remarkably, they stuck out of his mouth, leading to his nickname. Both were telling me how powerful the Japanese Army was and how the war would go on for a hundred years, so we would never get back to America again. I came right back at them and, with my limited knowledge of Japanese, claimed that Tokyo, Yokohama, and Kawasaki would be bombed off the map by American B-29 bombers, and the POWs would be back home in six months—I didn't know how close to the truth I was. But they sure got quiet, as though I had shaken them up.

In fact, at that time I was being wildly optimistic, while the prediction of the old boss and Fangs of a very long war seemed plausible—the daylight, B-29 bombing of Japanese factories had not been very successful so far. Although General MacArthur had invaded the Philippines on October 20, 1944, many months of fighting seemed to lay ahead there.

The task of invading and defeating Japan would take years and cost millions of lives if Japanese soldiers fought to the last man, as they had done thus far in losing island after island.

The next day these civilian Japs did not want to continue the argument, although I was more than ready. Such a discussion could not be held with the Japanese soldiers at the prison camp.

The following day B-29s sent us into the air-raid tunnel again for a couple of hours, but that was no evidence that my wild prediction of Japanese defeat would happen. A day later a sharply-dressed civilian showed up at the old boss's work site. He asked questions and walked around with the old man as though he owned the place, and indeed he was the top boss of Showa Denko Chemical Works. I liked seeing a civilian in good clothes—even a Jap—since the civilians we usually saw were mostly in rags.

XIV

An Easier Mood

January 17, 1945, to February 25, 1945

Every now and then one of the details I directed under the old boss put me on the spot. On January 17, 1945, it was Sgt. William McCool. He was a short, stocky man who had become somewhat fluent in Japanese. Now he had just come back to work after being off for a few days with a minor injury. Hungry from being on half-rations, McCool stole some rice and was cooking it when a camp guard caught him. The guard reported this to the old boss. But when he and Guchi asked McCool where he had found the rice, he explained—or appeared to explain—in a torrent of poor Japanese. They just laughed and joked about the fact they couldn't figure out where the rice had come from.

At camp after supper, Mac and I were called into the office of Kondo, the interpreter, who at times could be easygoing. But Little Henry was also there, and he could be nasty. Yet both of them had bought the joke about not finding the rice Mac had cooked. Back in the barracks, Mac and I slapped ourselves on the back because we had gotten away with something—he for cooking the rice and I for letting him do it.

Yet a couple days later, when I had the day off, McCool nudged me awake from a long nap to tell me he had gotten into trouble again. This time, instead of cooking the rice himself, he had gotten Fangs to do it for him and others while they were working. That was going to be OK except that the rice had become cold by the time the men came back to eat it. Then when they started to heat it up themselves, the same guard who had caught McCool before walked up. The next day the guard came around and slapped McCool and his buddies, Wilkins, Silverman, and Reidinger.

How things had changed! If McCool and the others had been caught cooking rice our first winter here, they'd be dead—or wish they were after they had been beaten for hours, or perhaps days! Had the scary appearance of the huge, high-flying B-29s made the Japs worry about future accounting for our treatment? But such hopeful thoughts would have given way to darker ones if we had known of the massacre of 140 American and Filipino prisoners on Palawan Island off the Philippines the month before.* This atrocity was not random but consistent with Japanese military orders not to let any prisoner be rescued. Thus it was probably related to General MacArthur's landing on Leyte Island on October 20, 1944—the first blow in taking back the Philippines.

But life among the group of Americans assigned to the old man's Showa Denko work site went on swimmingly. Each morning we gathered in the shelter shack where I assigned jobs to my crew of 40 or so POWs. Then I proceeded to assign targets for pilfering while McCool, with his Japanese language ability, engaged the old boss and Fangs in distracting conversation.

The Japanese laborers at the factory were used to seeing us around—especially me, since the old boss had sent me as a messenger-boy all over the place on one errand or another. So I could enter an office or building without challenge. If I found some soap or good-looking clothing inside a building, I noted it for later pickup, or if the way was clear I just walked off with it. When there was opportunity to communicate, we steered McCool to where we had stashed the loot. It was then up to Mac to trade with the Koreans for cigarettes or anything he could get. Then we split the cigarettes. The Koreans didn't seem to have much more freedom than we did, although they were not POWs. But they were excellent pilferers and shrewd traders. They were conscripted from Korea, a Japanese colony.

It was risky business going into buildings that we had no business being in, but the standard procedure if caught was to look stupid and ask, "Where is the latrine?" We usually got away with it by managing to look as stupid as POWs were supposed to be. Although some got caught, nothing was ever proved. I escaped all scrutiny—the old boss wouldn't believe that I would let any of my crew steal! I always saw that the tasks he assigned were done in a reasonable time. He liked me and often remarked, "Number eighteen is okay." So no report of our pilfering scheme ever got back to camp.

This routine of ours went on for some time, but finally the Japs were

*Spector, Eagle Against the Sun, *page 527.*

so cleaned out of anything worthwhile that the gain was not worth the effort's risk. Back at camp it had been fun smoking Japanese cigarettes in front of the guards who couldn't get any.

Air-raid alerts continued in the last days of January. On the 28th we kept shoveling coal through an alert at 10 A.M. As always, I liked the half-coolie lunch at noon—not as large as earlier but still larger than lunches received by other work details. The next day I added to my diet at camp by carrying food buckets for Murdock, since he had been sick for the previous few days—I weighed 145 pounds now, up from a low of 125 in January of 1943.

The next day 90 of us had an easy day shoveling coal. The coolies didn't yell at us to hurry as they used to two years before. We set our own pace and stopped and rested or talked whenever we felt like it. But the half-coolie lunch was practically nothing now. The coolies' own food shortage may have calmed them down. Even though the camp staff must have realized American bombers and submarines had disrupted food distribution, they were treating us better than before.

On another detail on January 31, we did very little work. The Japanese civilians were jabbering so fast and furious about the shortage of the factory food ration, they forgot we were there. So we just sat and listened, but there was no indication that they blamed us for the American blockade of Japan. I felt sorry for these poor people—this war was certainly not their fault.

After supper that night the guards passed out three Red Cross parcels for each four men. Kondo asked us to donate enough milk, sugar, and coffee to the Japanese chaplain for him to have a full can of each. I didn't donate because I figured the Japanese officers could take care of the chaplain. Yet Kondo's willingness to dispense the Red Cross parcels to us when the general population lacked food was another sign of the better treatment we were getting in early 1945.

There were a few air-raid alerts in the first part of February, and then two B-29s flew over us on February 14. The next day two other B-29s kept us in the Showa Denko air-raid tunnel for two hours. But on February 16 a series of air raids kept us idle for most of the day after we were late in reaching our normal work site because of an alert. During that day we saw lots of Navy dive bombers and B-29s giving Tokyo hell about three miles away. It was the best and biggest raid I had ever seen—keep it up, Yanks!

We learned after the war that planes from Navy carriers struck Tokyo at this time, while B-29s struck the Mitsubishi Engine Works at Nagoya. These strikes were launched to support the Marine landing on Iwo Jima on February 19—to forestall Japanese fighter aircraft from leaving Japan to defend Iwo Jima.

At camp that day I brought Ed Lubiewski's chow to him in the hospital section—Dr. Curtin had cut a wart off his foot. Still trying to satisfy my hunger, I took Murdock's fire guard watch for the hour before midnight to pay for the extra chow he had given me.

The next day the sirens blew as we fell out to work, so Kondo told us we were to stay in. But then my old boss showed up and asked for our detail, so we went anyway. In recent days Kondo had held back the old boss's work group for an hour after the boss had slapped one of our work crew. Now the old boss was insisting we report on time. He had never before come to camp and asked for us to come. Now Kondo had to give in and let us go. Was the military losing prestige and clout after the appearance of the B-29s and Japanese defeats on island after island that brought the Americans closer to Japan itself?

There were no alerts for a day, but on February 19 eight or ten B-29s bombed Tokyo. The next day the siren sounded at 7 A.M., but we went to work anyway on a very cold day. That night I went on sick call and stayed in the next day with an infected finger. It was so cold in the barracks that Sgt. John Seres and I had to "bunk up" together with all our clothes on to get warm enough to sleep. I was back at work the next day during an all-day snow. For once I wasn't hungry enough to eat everything at lunch, so I gave one of my crew a cake to carry my chow bucket the next day.

The snow stopped the night of February 22. The next morning there was ten inches on the ground—more than the Javanese had ever seen. They were just like kids, playing, laughing, and washing each other's faces in it.

Four days later, transportation was still tied up all along Tokyo Bay, but our work was close by and the sun was shining, so they sent us off to work. But I had no shoes, since I had turned in my worn-out ones and had received no replacements. Navy Lt. Carney lent me his Oxfords, but my feet were soon soaked anyway in walking to work. Carney usually kept himself busy taking roll, making announcements, etc. On December 1 he had caught me asleep on fire-watch—I was glad it wasn't Shiozawa.

XV

Incendiary Bombing

February 25, 1945, to June 1, 1945

On February 25 we saw carrier planes buzzing the tall chimneys of Kawasaki close by and then stayed in the tunnel for an hour. A heavy snow started at noon and was still coming down at 2 P.M. when six B-29s flew right through it to bomb Tokyo.* I was all gassed up because I ate so much food the day before. My lack of appetite a few days earlier had been short-lived.

On March 9, B-29s raided Tokyo again, starting at 11 P.M. In the next few days, Gilbert, who could read and speak Japanese, learned some details of the raid from a Tokyo newspaper that was furnished by a friendly guard. The B-29s had come in single file and dropped fire bombs upwind from the city. The wind carried the bombs to the center of Tokyo and fanned the fires that the bombs had started. Large fires were still burning at dawn, and the city smoldered for two days.† We learned this from Gilbert, who had ingratiated himself with two Japanese guards, who let him read news reports of the raid on Tokyo. Gilbert was our best source of news because he could read and speak Japanese.

---

*We learned after the war that 172 B-29 bombers fire-bombed Tokyo on February 25, burning out a square mile of urban area. Nothing like that had been accomplished before. It was the conclusive test of fire-bombing the mostly wooden structures of Japanese cities, a practice which the U.S. Army Air Corps had urged be adopted by Washington since the beginning of the year. Birdsall, Saga of the Flying Superfortress, pages 167–168.

†After the war the Japanese Government reported 78,660 casualties and 15.8 square miles of burnt-out urban area in Tokyo from this raid. U.S. records show that 334 B-29s took off for the raid. Comparably large fire-bombing raids on the Japanese cities of Nagoya, Osaka, and Kobe followed on March 11, 13, and 19. Birdsall, Saga, page 182.

A few days later Gilbert's two friendly guards invited Gilbert and me to their quarters to listen to foreign news broadcasts. I never did it again because I was afraid these guards would be found out. Then both guards, Gilbert, and I would be punished severely. But Gilbert kept on going and was not caught.

At this time we believed that the residential sections of Tokyo and elsewhere were being burned out because many houses had lathes or drill presses that contributed to the war effort by producing items such as bearings. Thus, destruction of homes was necessary. What a shame that these helpless people were being burned out of their homes. I bet they were regretting they ever bombed Pearl Harbor.

Oddly enough, Red Cross parcels were getting to us without anything being taken, and the galley was giving us larger rations. Anger at the bombing was not being transferred to us at the camp or work sites.

A few days later I really lucked out—Bucktooth, the camp quartermaster, issued me a new pair of 9 EE U.S. Army shoes that fit perfectly.

But things were getting bad for the Japanese civilians. They received only three cigarettes a day after the March 9 raid on Tokyo destroyed its main cigarette factory. On March 19 I noticed a lot of civilians in Kawasaki were evacuating—after seeing what had happened to Tokyo. Feeling the same way, I got my gear ready to evacuate instead of going to muster on March 19. Then during the four hours after midnight on April 4 I sat in terrible suspense, watching the spectacular sight of a heavy raid only a mile from us. All dressed with my pack on my lap, I felt like a sitting duck that couldn't fly.

In late March the Japanese Army guards were transferred—probably to take part in defending against an American landing. They were replaced by green Home Guards. We could have been worried, because the Japanese staff had told us more than once that all of us would be executed in case of an American landing on Japan's main islands in order to free the guards for fighting the invasion.* Yet now the guards had left, and there seemed to be no change in the better mood and treatment of us at camp and the factories since mid–January, as I had noticed.

The answer may have been that we were too useful where we were, since all the able-bodied young men working in the factories had long since been drafted into the Army. All that was left to keep production going were old men, children, and us.

*In radio messages between April 1942 and five days after Japan's surrender, on August 20, 1945, command headquarters in Tokyo consistently directed POW camp commanders not to let any military prisoners or civilian internees be freed by Allied forces. Instead, the commanders were ordered "not to allow the escape of a single one, to annihilate them all, and not to leave any traces." Holmes, Unjust Enrichment, page xiv.

The Army itself must have been getting very short on manpower. We knew the Japanese must have suffered heavy losses in capturing and losing the Philippines and islands all the way to New Guinea, as well as in fighting in Southeast Asia and fighting in China since 1931. Currently the defense of Iwo Jima would mean the total loss of Japanese troops there, and the U.S. invasion of Okinawa on April 1 would finally wipe out the entire garrison of 70,000 there.*

Yet life went on at Kawasaki much as before. The Javanese put on a show for Easter, which entertained both us and the Japanese staff. On April 7 the hungry Marine, Don Armstrong, got into trouble again—this time he stayed in the sack when he was supposed to be on fire guard. Kondo didn't slap Armstrong very hard. Yet Armstrong's face blew up like a balloon—earlier terrible beatings from stealing food may have taken a permanent toll.

On April 13 we learned of President Roosevelt's death the day before, and the Japs were very happy about it. Lt. Hayashi, the newly-arrived camp commander, refused permission for us to conduct prayers, although it was customary for us to have a brief prayer upon the death of one of us. Hayashi declared that Roosevelt was Japan's enemy and he was glad to see him die. Then Fangs at our regular work site tried to tell me that Japanese aircraft had bombed the White House and killed the President. When I laughed in his face and told him he was crazy, he got quite angry. I could get away with talking like that to a civilian—especially there, where I was the old boss's favorite worker and senior noncom.

After an alarm for a local raid at 9:20 P.M. on April 15, we grabbed our belongings and headed for the docks—where we had worked on so many urgent unloadings. I was almost there when I heard a familiar voice ahead, "Herb! Come under here with me." I Looked around for who was calling, and then heard the same voice coming from one of the ship-loading cranes, which sat on steel platforms that stood about head high above the dock. Underneath this platform I found my old friend, Ed Lubiewski. We stayed under there during the four-hour raid by 300 B-29s that set all of Kawasaki afire—the incendiary bombs seemed to float toward the docks but never reached us, so none of us were injured. Production at Kawasaki never completely recovered. No enemy aircraft challenged the raid, but the anti-aircraft fire was very heavy. I saw five of the B-29s shot down. It

---

*Spector, Eagle Against the Sun, *page 540. Also in his drive toward the Philippines, General MacArthur had evaded and isolated 220,000 enemy troops—many greatly disheartened because they would never be able to fight. William Manchester,* American Caesar, *page 373.*

tore my heart out to visualize the flaming death the crew members were to meet upon crashing, or the torture they would face if they survived the crash.* After roll call we took our belongings back to camp and went to bed.

The next day there were no work details for lack of electric power in Kawasaki. Water was so short that in the afternoon I was on a five-man detail that hauled water from another part of town. On the way we passed the rambling Nippon Steel Works. It was the primary target last night and was still burning that evening.

The following day there was still no work, so we spent the morning discussing how much longer the war could go on. Our guesses varied from one month to one year. Naturally cautious, I hoped we would be home for Christmas.†

In the afternoon I went on a work detail to haul furniture. Since there was only one guard to watch us, we all managed to sneak into another part of the warehouse and steal all the raw rice we could carry. I got enough Saigon rice for eight rations, which I shared with Ed. Because of a vegetable shortage, the galley was issued two cases of Red Cross food parcels, so we had barley, corned beef, cornstarch, and chocolate for supper. Reconnaissance aircraft flew over Kawasaki three times during the day— to assess the damage or photograph the next target.

There were still no regular work details, so some of the men went out to work on the vegetable garden. Of those, a few strayed over to the rice warehouse, looking for a rice haul. But they were caught and sent back to camp before noon. Kondo and the guards slapped the culprits, who were then made to stand at attention until one of them would confess to being the first to enter the locked warehouse. Not wanting to betray the guilty

---

*The summary from the War Crimes Trials concluded that after torture, airmen were usually murdered. The Yokohama tribunal convicted Col. Yoshinao Sato, Chief of Air Intelligence and Air Defense at West HQ, Fukuoka, Japan, of killing eight American flyers on each of three days, and seventeen on another day, by bayoneting and beheading. He was condemned to death but not executed. Thus he was in line to be released by 1958. Ginn, Sugamo Prison, pages 139–40. E. Bartlett Kerr, Surrender and Survival (William Morrow, 1985), page 268, reports that probably more than 200 American fliers were killed or executed after coming down.

†All of us would have been more gloomy if we had realized the new tactic the Japanese Army had adopted against U.S. forces invading Okinawa—not to waste men contesting the landing but to retire into caves to make a kamikaze stand. Thus the inevitable American victory would take longer and cost more lives. To overcome kamikaze fighting on the main islands of Japan would require years of combat. William Manchester, Goodbye, Darkness (Bantam, 1979). Some Japanese-occupied caves had been used as tombs so when the Marines burned out the enemy, they damaged many Okinawan graves. William H. Thomas, unpublished manuscript, Indianapolis.

one, they stood at attention until midnight when, tired and hungry, they figured out a solution. DeGroot, a Dutchman, would confess—in return for three cigarettes from each member of the group. Expecting something bad would happen to him, we saw Kondo take DeGroot into his office, but in a few minutes he came out unruffled and told us Kondo and the new top sergeant had slapped him around a little bit and bellowed at him, but then had given him back his stolen rice and treated the whole thing as a big joke.

Four days after the big raid, the Showa Denko Chemical Works called for 50 of us. They gave us brooms and told us to sweep the streets of the factories. We dispersed to do the sweeping but soon realized the factories were practically empty, and there was no guard to watch us. We went through every office we could get into and stole everything of value or that we might be able to trade with the Koreans for cigarettes. Lots of things we took were of no value, but we took them just for the fun of it. It was exhilarating to be able to wander around without anyone watching us. We went into an air-raid shelter at 10 A.M. for an hour. Afterwards we learned that two American fighters from a carrier had strafed the gun positions on top of the power plant and shot down two Japanese training planes.

But the next day water and power had been restored at the camp, and Showa Denko was back to almost complete operation. However, some civilians had not returned from the hills. Fangs told us his house had been burned down during the April 15 raid—too bad. A day later, one B-29 flew directly overhead—so low it scared the hell out of us. We could see the fly-boys looking out of the windows—lucky devils.

Kondo told us at 7 P.M. roll call that he would be leaving tomorrow. Then the Javanese put on a musical program for him. He was a capable interpreter who had been given a lot of authority by Lt. Saito and the new camp commander, Lt. Hayashi. We thought we might miss Kondo because he had a more balanced personality than the rest of the staff—especially Shiozawa. Kondo had restrained the guards from punishing us from time to time. But now he warned us that there would be a lot of shakedowns after he left. Was he trying to discourage the heavy pilfering that had been going on?

On April 27 I went to sick call because one of my eyes was watering. Doc Curtin told me it was caused by acid fumes and put some drops in it. But two days later there had been no improvement. This time Doc ordered me to another work detail because of the fumes at the work site of the friendly old boss, where I had been going off and on for two years. But my eye problem did not affect my appetite.

On May 3 we had pickled seaweed for the first time. The men in our eating section didn't like it; but when I tried it, I liked it so much I devoured the servings of three others while my friends said, "Zincke will eat anything!"

Although the air raids had not been close to us since the fire bombing of Kawasaki, finally, on May 9, Kondo—who had not left after all— got around to listing the clothing we should have for an emergency move. We had been eager to move for months—this waiting and wondering just when our bombers would level our camp was beginning to tell on all of us. I became depressed—partly because I could no longer go to the work site of the friendly old boss because of the acid fumes there. When we heard that Germany had surrendered on May 7, we remembered the earlier threats of our execution—so the guards would be free to repel the expected landing, which could now be augmented by American troops from Europe.

By May 16 I was really down in the dumps. I was so damn disgusted and discouraged that I could have killed myself or some damn Jap to break the monotony. Faith and hope had been all we had to cling to, and sometimes I wondered if that would be enough to keep me going. I went to bed early to sleep it off, since I was in a dangerous mood. But I felt better the next day. I didn't mind the new work of cleaning up the machine shop where I had been assigned after Doc Curtin said the fumes at my old work site were too much for my eyes. An air raid kept us in a shelter from noon to 1:30 P.M.

A couple of days later Ed Lubiewski fell off a ladder while working in the machine shop and hurt himself badly enough to land in the hospital section. Kondo was there when Ed was brought back to camp. That evening at roll call Kondo read a special order from Lt. Hayashi, which stated that we were not to do any dangerous work on our details. What a surprise!

This sudden concern for us may have reflected a changing attitude among the top levels of the Japanese Government. The new prime minister, Admiral Suzuki Kantaro, who took office in April 1945, claimed later that he had tried to end the war by persuading the Soviet Union to mediate between the U.S. and Japan. If his peace policy had succeeded, the treatment of American POWs in Japan would have been open to world scrutiny.

Early on May 19, Gilbert, who knew Japanese, overheard Kondo talking about a big shakedown that evening. But no one knew what the Japs would be looking for. Finally someone remembered that we had stolen a lot of soft soap two weeks before and smuggled it into camp in baggy pants. We had gotten rid of most of it by trading with the Koreans for cigarettes. Now we got rid of the rest of it, so Kondo's shakedown that night was fruitless. Afterwards we found that some of the Koreans had been caught with some of the soap we had traded to them—as we thought might happen.

The next day at evening roll call Kondo told us that if we needed anything for evacuation, we should not steal it from each other but pick it up at the factories. It sounded like evacuation was likely. The lack of consideration for the factories fell in with Kondo's earlier order not to do any dangerous work at the work sites.

Six days after we had stolen the soap and traded some to the Koreans, the dreaded Kempetai, the Japanese secret police, came around looking for the stolen soap—there must have been something else involved to bring in the Kempetai. They couldn't find any soap because we wouldn't even talk to them, although they tried to be friendly. We were also careful not to say anything to each other because most of them understood and spoke perfect English. They soon gave up and went away.

I woke up with a jolt at 0130 A.M. to hear the sirens blowing like mad. The Japanese were caught flat-footed—the raid had already started. The sky was overcast, and the B-29s came in low at different altitudes, confusing the wildly firing anti-aircraft gunners. Except for fire-fighting and rice-drying details, all of us evacuated the camp and gathered under the steel and cement platforms that supported the cranes used to unload coal ships and freighters. There, on a peninsula jutting out into Tokyo Bay, I again stood with my friend Ed watching the raid. I did not fear the fire-sticks because they fell slowly and burned brightly, so they could be avoided if necessary. But the heavy nose weights fell at a terrific speed after the bomb burst in the air. We could not see them and knew where they hit only when we heard a heavy splash in the bay or a dull thud on land.

The noise of the bombers, the bombs bursting in the air, and the guns firing atop the power plant would put the fear of God into the bravest man. It was a terrifyingly beautiful sight. The raid was a complete success—I saw none of our planes hit or shot down. The B-29s kept coming until 4:30 A.M., but we stayed under the cranes until dawn. There were said to be 240 B-29s over the Tokyo area in this raid—I wouldn't doubt it, as they were thick as flies. Just to think! At about 5,000 feet were free Americans who saw the American flag every day!

At camp we found that the brave fire-fighting crew, helped by the rice-drying group, had managed to put out numerous small fires set by strips of flaming jelly and save the Mitsui Madhouse. Water was useless, so they smothered the flames with dirt and sand. In the end they saved our camp. It was a mess, but we still had a "house," which was more than the Japs living near our camp had—their houses were burned to the ground. Later Mitsui Company gave us each a box of black tea and a little horseradish for saving their building—our barracks.

Roll Call at 7:00 showed we had no losses among those ordered to evacuate or those who stayed and fought the fires. Then we all turned to repairing and cleaning up the camp. Later a half-dozen of us, whose job had been handling and loading bombs and ammunition on American bombers, found enough parts to assemble a complete incendiary bomb. It was a new type to us, but we enjoyed figuring out together how it operated—a small class about which the guards showed no interest.

The next morning we did not go to work but spent all day talking about the raid and our slim chance of survival in future raids on the many industrial targets in this area. Last night's raid knocked out our electricity, so we had roll call at 7 P.M. and went to bed.

The day after next, May 25, another air raid pulled us out of bed at 11 P.M. Again we gathered under the crane platforms, but we were soon brought back to camp to stand by to fight possible fires. It turned out we were fairly safe, since the B-29s were bombing Tokyo. Nippon Steel seemed to be a main target—our boys dropped both fire and demolition bombs on its plants. The Japs were ready this time—the numerous anti-aircraft guns opened up with a terrific stream of fire. We lost at least six B-29s that I saw go down.*

Most of those went down in the bay, but one crashed in Kawasaki near the railroad station. It burned for about twenty minutes as it circled, while the crew tried to put out the flames. Finally the pilot must have realized the effort was hopeless because he power-dived into the ground. The explosion shook the ground where we stood. Tears came to my eyes to see those heroes give up their lives after such a brave struggle. Later the Japanese said that the crew was buried where they crashed, and that one member of the crew was a woman. We didn't believe either report—there wouldn't have been anything left of the crew to bury, and we knew damn well that no woman would be allowed to fly on such a dangerous mission. I suppose the Japs will believe anything, though. All Clear sounded at 2 A.M., but it was a long time before I could get the sight of the crashing bomber out of my mind and go to sleep.

After this raid on Tokyo, the attitude of the guards changed. Instead

---

The May 25 raid on Tokyo was the Army Air Corps' largest single mission against Japan. Seventeen square miles of Tokyo were destroyed, but there was a heavy loss of B-29s and their crews. Birdsall, Saga of the Superfortresses, *page 225.*

of standing around joking, their talk turned serious. In the next few days, a couple of them were missing. We concluded that they had taken to the hills or gone home on their own.

The next day a B-29 reconnaissance flight made us expect another heavy raid that night; but after a General Alarm at 11 P.M., there was no raid, so after waiting on the docks for two hours we went back to camp. A couple of days later Kondo posted a new fire-fighting detail, but luckily I was not on it.

At 8:50 A.M. on May 29 three blasts—meaning a local raid—sent us into the tunnel at Kosaka Soko. While nervously smoking, we could hear heavy bombing from the direction of Yokohama—it lay on Tokyo Bay south of us. It was a beautiful clear day when we entered the shelter; but when we emerged two hours later, the sky was black with smoke and dust, and Yokohama was burning fiercely.

Later one of the guards at camp said he heard over the radio that there were 500 B-29s and 100 P-51 fighters over Yokohama, and both incendiary and demolition bombs were dropped. Despite heavy anti-aircraft fire, no aircraft was known to have been shot down—much to the disgust of the same talkative guard. The P-51 fighters must have provided good protection. Two days later a single B-29 flew high over Yokohama, taking pictures of what was left of it.

XVI

Sgt. Mizuno

June 1, 1945, to July 1, 1945

On June 1 we were glad to see Lt. Hayashi, the camp commander, leave. A young officer replaced him, but Sgt. Mizuno now ran the camp. He permitted work details to construct slit trenches covered by earth on the Mitsui waterfront. He let other men apply a dirt-covering to the trenches that had been dug outside the back gate of the barracks. Besides, Mizuno immediately stopped the guards from stomping up and down in the barracks during the night—Hayashi had wanted to remind us we were prisoners. It didn't matter that air-raid alerts were already interrupting our sleep every night or so.

Daytime guard patrols through the barracks had annoyed us for a long time, but the guards were never able to catch us with any loot because we had a warning system. The first man on the bottom floor who saw a guard enter or look in the barracks' door or window would insert "red light" at a normal tone in a conversation he was in or would start. Others would pick up the signal and pass it on. Within seconds, everyone downstairs and upstairs had the warning and had time to hide stolen rice, soap, or cigarettes under his blanket or among his clothes. When the guard left the floor, All Clear was inserted into many conversations in a like manner. Nobody betrayed the system to the guards. Even Kondo, the interpreter, never told them. Once, though, Kondo came into the barracks and yelled, "'Red Light!' Very clever, you Yanks!"

On June 5 Sgt. Mizuno told us that we would only work at the docks now, since we were not needed at the factories. Many of them had been shut down by the bombing. Those of us not needed at the docks would work on bomb shelters, gardens, or other odd jobs around the camp. That same day "high brass" from the Japanese Imperial War Cabinet inspected us. We hoped this top attention was an effort to make sure that our condition would look all right if peace came and we came under international inspection.

The next day I was at work building an air-raid shelter. We set our own pace, as there were no guards to bother us. A number had drifted away after the massive Tokyo raid. Sgt. Mizuno told us to wash our woolen trousers and blouses and leave them on our shelves rather than turn them in—tying in with the latest rumor that this midnight was the deadline for Japanese surrender. I'd wanted to believe the rumor but didn't.

That day the trials of summer began. A work detail pulled off all the bunk mats, cleaned them thoroughly, and sprinkled Japanese flea powder over them and the wooden sleeping platforms. But their efforts were in vain because I woke up the next morning to find red circles all over my body—I had slept naked, so the fleas had a feast.

After we stopped going to the factories we went in and out of the camp as we pleased without a guard, and nobody cared if we worked or not. Sgt. Mizuno didn't seem to care what we did, within reason. He, his young cousin (whom we called "Little Mizuno"), and the new quartermaster Hojami all spoke English as well, if not better, than the new interpreter, Yamazaki. The relationship between the Japanese staff and us warmed so much that I wondered if my more optimistic friends were right in thinking the war was over.

Each night for about two months I had had my Dutch knapsack packed and all my equipment handy to grab in case of a serious air raid. Every other night I put fresh water in my canteen. I was ready for a quick evacuation, as I had a hunch that our little vacation from air raids was about over and that all hell would break loose very soon. What a spot to be in! So damn helpless, and sitting right in the center of one of the most important industrial areas in Japan. We surely would have been a poor risk if we were trying to take out life insurance.

On June 8 I sat on my bunk waiting for the usual 7 P.M. roll call—only to find it had already been called at 6:15! Always something new at our "Mitsui Madhouse." It was also new that I was not beaten for missing roll call.

After 90 Javanese left camp on June 3, Sgt. Mizuno just gave up on using the remaining 40 on any regular work detail. Instead, he assigned them clean-up and odd jobs at camp. They were just no good to do work that required any perseverance. When told to work at something, they played dumb and said they didn't understand. The Americans often ended up doing their work on the docks rather than have the camp guards take it out on all of us.

The next day M/Sgt. Britton sent me with the new all–American 50-man dock detail to replace the Javanese who had now been assigned to camp work. On the dock Wallie Hewson and I unloaded coal from rail cars. We shoveled it into the center of the car so the overhead crane could scoop it up and drop the coal into the waiting barge in the bay. Our buddy, "Red" Westervelt, operated the crane, so when we wanted to take a break, we signaled Red to lower the crane shovel for us to sit on.

At about eleven that morning, Wallie and I were standing at the far end of the car, waiting for Red to pick up a load. While I was looking out at the bay, the crane shovel hit me in the back and flipped me over the end of the car. I landed with my left leg on the coupling between the cars. I thought I had broken my leg, but the only damage seemed to be two deep cuts, which were bleeding badly.

Red immediately climbed off his crane and came to me—sorry but relieved that I wasn't in worse shape. He said the controls had jammed so the shovel went the wrong way. He wrapped up my leg, and a roving guard took me to the mess hall. At 1 P.M. I finally reached camp, where Doc Curtin cleaned and bandaged my leg. Then I was back in the hospital section, next to Ed Lubiewski again. He was still recuperating from falling off a ladder on May 18. A head cold had put me in the hospital section with Ed on May 28.

The next day, despite my accident, I was able to get down to the shelter of the crane platforms when a General Alarm sounded at breakfast. The same thing happened the following day—40 carrier planes were said to have made the raid. Ed Lubiewski and I carried our gear out of camp during air raids in a wheelbarrow Ed had stolen. We took turns pushing, since neither of us was in very good shape.

The night of June 11 the Japanese staff, now all enlisted men under Sgt. Mizuno, had a sake party and gave us some. But Richards, the crane operator, vomited all over the upstairs—they gave him the next day off.

At roll call on June 13, Navy Lt. Carney criticized us for not volunteering for details around the camp on our days off from dock work. But in the absence of tight Japanese control, camp work had been accomplished by the reward of extra food. When such reward seemed unlikely, nobody volunteered. Carney also threatened to report us to Sgt. Mizuno for punishment if we didn't get to roll call on time in the morning—some of us have been late because we took time to wash. All of a sudden, Carney thought he could act like the captain of a ship. But his attitude was putting the men in a rebellious mood.

The next day, on June 14, we had early roll call at 5 A.M. A coal ship had come in that the Japs were in a hurry to unload—apparently fearful that it would be a prime target moored there along the Mitsui docks. Now Sgt. Mizuno even sent out thirty Javanese, along with 20 Americans. He warned the Javanese that there would be retaliation back at camp if they didn't work well. The Javanese responded, and the coal was unloaded by the end of the day.

Both Lubiewski and I were now well enough to go, but I had to go back on sick call at noon because my leg became swollen from walking around so much. I had to stay quiet, although I hated to lie down all the time and do nothing.

A couple of days later, during a midnight air raid, a camp guard caught Ed and me smoking under a crane platform and took our POW numbers. We didn't know what he would do about it. That morning 95 men went out to unload coal. Since all able-bodied men had gone out working, I went ahead and cleaned the wash rack at the end of the chow line—I could do that without bothering my bad leg. It was the hospital section's turn to get the extra burned rice, so I managed to get quite full for a change.

On June 17 the Japanese civilian bosses complained to Sgt. Mizuno that the prisoners were not unloading coal like they used to. That was so—their passive resistance came mainly from not getting coolie lunches or cigarettes. Our men told me they just sat around in the hold and talked and laughed at the civilians who were trying to get them to work. At camp Sgt. Mizuno didn't seem to care how much work was done, so long as we filled out the daily work details. But unloading also had been drastically slowed because the coolies weren't working anymore on account of the air raids. So only the Koreans and POWs were left to unload the coal ships.

I was soon back at work and was shocked when we were all sent to a wooden mess hall during daylight raids. We sat there helpless, with the windows closed—waiting for a fire bomb to set the building on fire. There were no bomb shelters or comparatively safe places to go, and we were in particular danger because the coal docks were such an excellent military target. We hoped for an air raid that night that would sink the ship being unloaded and blow the coal docks to hell. That might be the only way we would get to move—for the docks to be destroyed. But our hopes for a move rose when Brontz, a Dutchman, returned from Shinagawa Hospital—supposedly in time for the camp's move around July 1. We feared more heavy bombing soon.

The next day, while we were eating lunch, a general drove up to inspect our camp. At that moment the General Alarm blew as a B-19 flew over at 30,000 feet. The general took one look, and he and his staff got back in their car and drove off. I guess they thought Kawasaki was not very safe.

Chet Krawieki, our cobbler, had a run-in with a guard who tried to take some shoe nails from him. When Chet refused to give him any, the guard tried to make Chet stand at attention and bow. Then Chet cussed him out and walked away. But when the guard reported the incident, Lt. Mori, the new camp commander, stuck up for Chet, since the nails were camp property. Mori, speaking perfect English, told Chet to be more polite when speaking to the guards and then dismissed the case! I hate to think of what would have happened to Chet if he had done that the first winter we were here.

We heard that the 90 Javanese who left camp to work in a copper mine and carbon factory were being treated badly by the civilians, received poor food, and worked very hard. This news made us realize that our camp would be hard to beat, except for its dangerous location. This mood seems to have spurred the men to finish unloading the coal ship the following day.

Mr. Kondo, our former interpreter, was in camp and said he thought the war would be over in a month or two. After a General Alarm but no raid, I got to talking to Little Mizuno, Sgt. Mizuno's cousin. He took me to his office where he told me that fifty B-29s were dropping fire bombs on three places up north. Blackie Young, the crane operator, and a couple of others joined us to listen to the radio account of the raid, while Little Mizuno interpreted the report and showed us the location of the raids on his map. It was very interesting, but soon the guard made us turn out the light. As we left for bed, Little Mizuno gave us each a cigarette.

After roll call on June 20, the dock detail fell out to march to work at 7:30 A.M. as usual. But "Smiley," the civilian boss, was not at the gate to march them to work. Five minutes later, Smiley showed up, but Sgt. Mizuno kept the men in the barracks and told Smiley he could come back and get them at 9 A.M. Smiley stalked away, hiding his fury behind an impassive face in typical Japanese fashion. Three days before, Mizuno had pretty much ignored complaints by the dock bosses that the POWs weren't working well.

I still was not working, but at sick call that day I found that my leg had just about healed. After lunch I took a small detail to the garden to pick Japanese lettuce. When we brought it back to camp, I asked Sgt. Mizuno for some cigarettes for the men, and he gave us each two.

About this time Raymond Chambers of the Coast Artillery, who bunked next to me, developed large boils on his face and neck. But when

Doc Curtin told him he was eating too much rice, Chambers declared he was going to eat as much rice as he could get. I had had no boils so far, but had lots of pimples and blackheads, probably because of few baths and little soap.

After lunch on June 25, the three blasts for a local alarm followed the General Alarm so quickly that I had to really hurry to load Ed Lubiewski's, Zalme's, and my gear on the wheelbarrow and wheel it down to the crane platforms. I was just getting my wind back when All Clear sounded. I was really pooped by the time I had gotten the loaded wheelbarrow back to camp because I had been laid up so long with my bad leg. We learned that the alarm was triggered by thirty carrier planes, which headed to the north.

The mosquitoes had driven me to using mosquito netting at night. Now the flies also were making themselves at home in the barracks, since we had no screens. They were awful. Everyone who did not go on details one day was given a fly swatter. That was fun, but there was no end to it. The next day each of us had a quota of 75 flies before lunch. Nobody missed lunch.

I didn't hear the alarm at 1 A.M. on June 29, but Chambers woke me. Then I went outside and sat for an hour looking at the beautiful, star-lit sky—thinking of home and whether I would ever see it. The next afternoon my morale was slipping again—I wondered what would happen to us and whether our effort to keep going was really worth it. When I started brooding like that, there was only one thing I could do—I lay down and went to sleep. Thank God I could go to sleep when I was in this mood. As always, I woke up refreshed and ready for another six months. These days, that was how we all answered the question of "How much longer?"

Now a good rumor cheered me up—we were to move up north. We had been hearing "moving rumors" since we arrived over two years ago, but maybe this was the real thing. The next day everyone had become so excited about leaving that they cooked the raw rice they had stolen so as not to lose it if we moved suddenly. I was skeptical but cooked mine too.

Part of the "move" rumor was that 62 British, Americans, and Canadians were to arrive before we left. Their actual arrival on June 30 brought an amazing boost to our morale—not only the prospect of moving but the opportunity to see and talk with some new people. There was lots of laughing and back-slapping, as though we were brothers who had not seen each other for years.

They had been working at a flour warehouse and so were a good deal heavier than we were. Most of them had been captured at Guam, Wake Island, or from merchant marine ships taken in the South Pacific.

Not all of the camp were moving—the newcomers were to continue

to work at the flour warehouse, and some old-timers would keep work-
ing at the coal docks. But I got to move from this dangerous spot. Sgt.
Mizuno also was to leave—probably not a good break for those staying.
Yet the new flour detail might help with the food supply.

On July 1 those of us leaving turned in our bowl bags, mosquito nets,
forks, raincoats, and factory clothing, and then mustered over on the Mitsui lot. It was a shakedown to see what we were taking with us, but the
inspection was so haphazard that I could have had a Browning Automatic
Rifle without their noticing it. After a good supper, we had a song-fest—
part of it consisting of solos by my friend Ed Lubiewski, who had a very
good voice. We also enjoyed the comedy acts put on by two senior Dutch
NCOs, Mensink and Lockerman.

XVII

Hidatchi

July 2, 1945, to July 17, 1945

On July 2, 61 Americans and 38 Javanese marched out of Camp No. 2 and passed by blocks of burnt-out buildings before we reached the railroad station. I hadn't realized how little was still standing in our area. But our barracks had been saved so far by our firefighters.

After boarding the train for Tokyo at 8:30 A.M., we soon were riding past the terrible devastation and ruins of the center and heart of Japan. What had been beautiful hotels and business buildings were burned down or thoroughly gutted. Even though we were their enemy, I couldn't help feeling sorry for them. We changed trains in Tokyo—the station was undamaged and still in operation—and left at 11 A.M. I got a seat by the window and enjoyed looking at the farms and countryside as we traveled north—a welcome change in scenery after seeing the smoke and dirt of Kawasaki for the past 2 years.

A few men became sick from eating too much the previous night, but Dr. Kaufman, a Dutchman, gave them something that helped. At 4 P.M. we reached Hidatchi, about 90 miles north of Tokyo. B-29s had partially burned out the town and factories about a week before. We boarded a street car and rode about an hour to the factory where we were to work. We walked from the street car only a hundred feet or so to our camp, where we received another shakedown. We had roll call at 7 P.M. and then a supper of barley and rice mixture, daikon, and a little shredded lettuce—it was about the same food that we had had at the Mitsui Madhouse. But the wooden building was new and the latrine much better.

Ed Lubiewski and I managed to get bunking spaces next to each other,

134

while on my other side William Hoy bunked. The mattress mats were thicker than at Kawasaki, and I slept better. Another plus was good water pressure because the water came from higher in the mountains that rose behind us.

There were already 200 Javanese and Norwegians in the camp—they liked it pretty well there. The camp worked three shifts at the copper smelting furnaces up the gorge from our barracks—6 A.M. to 2 P.M., 2 P.M. to 10 P.M., and 10 P.M. to 6 A.M.

The next day the Japanese measured and weighed each of the newcomers. I was 6 feet 1 inches tall and weighed 145 pounds. Like the rest of the travelers, I lost over two pounds during the train and streetcar rides—it was hard to explain that much loss just from missing our usual lunch.

Rations were two-thirds normal because we were not working yet. But the Dutch, Javanese, and Norwegians agreed to share the reduction with us—darn decent of them I thought. That evening we had music and dancing—we were all becoming very good friends, and there was a feeling of fellowship that was lacking at the Mitsui camp. I hoped it would last.

On July 4 everyone stood at attention while, one by one, each of us reported to the camp commander by saluting and signing a paper swearing not to escape and to obey orders at both camp and factory. Then each man about-faced and marched back to his place in formation. The whole performance involved standing at attention for an hour and fifteen minutes. One man, O'Brien, stood so rigidly that he passed out. Lt. Kudeire, the commander, was very military, but the prisoners already there told us he was fair and left the management of the prisoners to the POW officers as long as they followed Japanese Army regulations. That was fine with me. The POW CO was a lanky Dutch Air Force captain named DeJager. The old-timers told us he was very energetic and took complete charge of the POWs.

A General Alarm sounded while we were eating lunch. Three blasts soon followed, so we hustled to get our belongings ready to evacuate, but a half-hour later we were still waiting to get out of there when All Clear sounded. I can only guess the Japs were slow to move after three blasts because they hadn't had any massive raids like we saw at Kawasaki.

I was curious to see the lay of the land around us, so I climbed up on the roof of the barracks where there were racks for drying clothes. Our camp lay at the bottom of a gorge, 1200 to 1500 feet deep, which ran five miles down to the sea. One-half mile up the gorge from us were large copper-smelting furnaces. The furnace complex covered a large area but had not been a target. The town itself, with oil refineries, had been hit, but the hydroelectric plant there was still furnishing power to the furnaces.

M/Sgt. Oricht called roll at our first regular muster, but the Japanese sergeant couldn't understand his report because of Oricht's heavy Polish accent—we could barely understand him ourselves. When Lt. Kudeire, the camp commander, received the garbled roll call, he was furious and demanded Oricht's replacement.

Grant Kendrick and Samuel Ramey were assigned to the kitchen because they were the most undernourished of us new men. The ex–rice dealers at Camp No. 2, Blackie Young and Richards, were feeling a pinch in their diet since they weren't able to cook stolen rice on their cranes as at Kawasaki. I used to be part of their distribution scheme, but was well satisfied with the food at Hidatchi.

On July 6 I began work on the 2 P.M. to 10 P.M. shift. We moved to new sleeping locations so everyone on the same shift could move in and out without disturbing members of another shift. After a quick shake-down, we walked a half-mile up to the furnaces—on a narrow road that was cut along the side of the gorge.

William Hoy and I worked on Furnace number 1, along with two Norwegians, who showed us the ropes. Our job was to push a four-wheeled cart to various hoppers of different kinds of ore and rock, which contained some copper, gold, silver, and other metals. After loading the cart, we dumped its contents into the roaring furnace. It took about a half-hour to fill the furnace, and then we could relax for an hour until the ore had burned down. Now and then we had to push the large clinkers that had formed out on the cement floor. Then we broke them down into small pieces with air hammers for re-smelting.

We were given heavy gloves and nose masks to screen out some of the dust and terrible gas fumes. We looked like Negroes by the end of our shift but had a good hot bath before we marched back to camp. On our way a heavy rain soaked us. We had some extra soup and greens but no rice because of a misunderstanding in the galley.

Three blasts at 11 P.M. resulted in a total blackout, but there was no evacuation—at Mitsui three blasts usually meant finding shelter under the crane platforms. I woke up several times in the night to find the camp blacked out—indicating a number of alerts.

The next day, after roll call, the mess sergeant passed out a loaf of bread to each of us. Whenever there was a surplus of bread, it was divided up in that way. The kitchen celebrated each man's birthday by giving him a large portion of burnt rice. A serving of blood sausage surprised us a few days later—this happened about once a month when a nearby slaughterhouse donated blood and entrails to the kitchen. Our cooks ground it up into very good sausages. All this food made us feel good. But we soon found out there was a big drawback to being at this camp.

It began the next day after a strenuous morning of drilling clinkers. Then at 12:30 P.M. three blasts warned of a local raid. But the damn stupid Japs at the furnace would not let us go to the shelters. No planes came over, so they put us back to work until 1 P.M. But then with our shift's work done for the day, they wouldn't let us bathe until All Clear sounded at 1:45 P.M.—an odd, selective compliance with the siren.

The next day at Furnace number 1 was easier because we didn't have to drill clinkers. Back at camp after lunch I sewed my old Staff Sergeant chevrons on my blue Red Cross jacket. It was an odd combination, but it made me feel good to wear my stripes, even though I was thousands of miles from the U.S.A.

More of the same attitude about air raids at Furnace number 1 on July 10—the factory boss put us to work at 6:30 A.M. even as carrier planes were flying overhead. But a half-hour later he heeded the warning of three blasts by sending us into a tunnel. Soon an All Clear sent us back to work, but the boss ignored three blasts at 8:00 A.M. and kept us working. When warning blasts sounded again at 11:00 A.M., he lined us up for muster and sent us back to work. These Japs have not seen a good bombing raid, so are slow and undecided as to what to do.

On July 12 we had an easy day at Furnace number 1—sweeping up with Frank Garcia, who sleeps next to me, and a Java boy. All shifts changed that day. We changed to 10 P.M., so for one time we returned from our old morning shift at 2 P.M. and had to go out at 10 P.M. the same day. But we were excused from evening roll call on the new shift, and the first night I had an easy clean-up detail. The next night was not so good.

It was a dark night, so we cautiously made our way up the narrow road carved along the gorge that led to Furnace number 1. We started work at 10 P.M. under the old civilian boss who was doing his bit for the war effort. An hour later the siren sounded for a raid that later was estimated to number 800 planes. The old boss stopped work and turned off the blower and lights. While the bombers rumbled overhead, he tried to take roll in the dark but gave up in disgust because we couldn't see well enough to line up properly. Not having experience with air raids, the confused Jap took us out in the pouring rain and led us down outside-stairs to the building's basement. In the limited space we had to crouch under the huge furnace. It sat on heavy iron stilts only four feet above the floor.

I was furious as I crouched there. The furnace could spill white-hot molten ore over us if exploded by a bomb's direct hit or jarred loose by a near miss. I slipped away in the dark and went to the rest shelter, where I slept off my anger until quitting time at 6:30 A.M.

When we straggled back to camp that morning, everyone else on the shift was also furious about what happened during the air raid. When we reported the situation to Captain DeJager, he requested a meeting with Cpl. Oto and the factory bosses. The Captain invited me to come to help make the case for our protection.

At the meeting, Cpl. Oto said he wanted to do something for us but he couldn't buck the factory bosses who had charge of our work. Captain DeJager said the same thing. After I had argued against this "stone wall" for an hour, I left in disgust and went to bed. But when I woke up, I found a new notice on the bulletin board that explained new air-raid procedures—after my departure Captain DeJager had convinced the Japs to adopt my most important proposal, that is, when three blasts sounded, we were all to leave the furnace buildings and assemble in front of the machine shop. But the notice did not include my idea that we should then proceed immediately to the mess hall—at least 100 feet from the furnace.

On July 14, when our shift reached the furnaces at 10 P.M., the ovens were all shut down, so we just started doing clean-up work. Then a General Alarm at midnight tested how serious the Japs were about our safety. Now the furnace boss immediately lined us up and told us to stand by before he took off at a run for a telephone. He soon returned and told us there was only one B-29 in the region but not over our area. Then he had us march to the mess hall, where we waited until All Clear at 3:30 P.M. What a contrast to the last alert! All in all, it was a good night for me because I kept one jump ahead of the boss who was looking for me after the All Clear signal.

The following night it wasn't an air raid that scared me, but my own clumsiness on the way to the furnaces. The narrow road up the gorge to the furnaces ran 50 feet above a swift stream. That evening a heavy rain had fallen and then stopped, but clouds blanketed the sky and kept us in total darkness as we headed up the road for the night shift. Two of our shift, William Hoy and Mailloux, slipped over the muddy edge of the road and were sliding down the canyon when they grabbed small bushes whose roots were strong enough to save them.

After the boys were pulled to safety, I became intent on staying on the safer side of the road. But I soon walked into the drainage ditch that lined that side—sinking into water up to my knees and tearing flesh off the palm of my hand and fingers. I staggered on to the furnaces, but an air-raid alert kept us in the mess hall most of the shift—sitting in the dark and listening to distant bomb explosions and more rain beating down on the roof. When All Clear sounded, we stayed where we were because even the guards were reluctant to leave. Back at camp the next day, Dr. Kaufman treated the gashes on my hand. But I didn't need to use my hand on the next shift because everyone had the day off for a camp program.

Lt. Kudeire, the camp commander, started the proceedings by thanking us for our hard work and telling us he expected more of the same. Then the camp band performed—we had two violins, four guitars, an accordion, a trumpet, and a bugle. The band played popular Dutch songs that featured Havinga, a young Dutchman who performed miracles of music on his violin. Then my friend Ed Lubiewski made a hit singing American songs, accompanied by the band. The 30 Japanese guests and staff clapped enthusiastically. In the middle of the afternoon we had a treat of coffee with milk and cheese bread—reawakening a yearning for stateside food. We had to wonder if the Japs were thinking about having happy prisoners to free in case they lost the war.

The end of the celebration brought a surprise and a laugh. After the music the Japanese guests were treated with a loaf of bread and rice and then shown around. They seemed particularly interested in the galley. Then, before they left the camp, the American mess sergeant reported a dozen loaves of bread missing. The guards shook down the guests and found five loaves of bread on the camp interpreter and three loaves on an officer, while the rest of the party, including the women, had one or two loaves concealed on their persons. Everyone in Japan must have been hungry. I had stolen plenty of food myself.

The next morning, July 17, three blasts interrupted roll call, and we fell out to hurry through chow. Then, as we were eating, one carrier plane flew over and fired a couple of bursts on the furnace buildings. When five more planes soon followed, I headed for the foxholes behind the barracks and jumped in with a splash—the frequent rains had almost filled them up with muddy water that came up to my waist. Meantime, the carrier planes had dropped a few light bombs among the factory buildings and started a fire. Then another aircraft came over very slowly and low enough for us to see the star insignia on the gull-shaped wings of the U. S. Navy Corsair. The Navy must have known we were there and flew the Corsair over to cheer us up. And our spirits were lifted, even though the raid had sent us into flooded foxholes. For a half-hour we could hear light bombs dropping in the Hidatchi factory area. After the planes had gone, we climbed out of the foxholes and waited in the barracks until All Clear sounded at 11:30 A.M. We couldn't figure out whether the lack of Japanese opposition to this small daylight raid meant that their defense forces were concentrating in the south to repel a landing on the main island of Kyushu or the war was winding down.

XVIII

Destruction of Hidatchi

July 18, 1945, to August 14, 1945

Just after midnight on July 18 I was awakened by terrific explosions. I lay for a second trying to hear the aircraft but heard nothing. Then a noise like a rushing express train followed by a deafening explosion brought me to my feet. As I hurriedly dressed, I realized the U.S. Navy was shelling our area. In the pitch-black dark I felt my way around the barracks to where I could look toward the ocean, but could see no horizon—only blackness. But soon we saw a flash of light that was followed by the rushing sound and explosion that I had heard in my bunk. Then other flashes came from the same spot—each followed by the frightening rushing sound and tremendous explosion. At first we worried that the nearby furnaces were a target, but when none of the shells came very close to us, we just enjoyed the show. Although the shelling lasted about a half-hour, there was no return fire nor aircraft to challenge the cruiser or battleship. We all thought there might be a landing party because the water was deep close to shore, making it easy for large ships to shell enemy forces at close range. But everything stayed quiet, so we went back in the barracks and hung up our clothes, which had been soaked by rain while we were watching.

That morning all three shifts walked up the narrow, muddy road to the furnaces—staying carefully in the middle of the road. But the civilian management did not want us because there were not enough bosses to supervise us—they had all left for the mountains farther inland. When we got back to camp, lots of civilians were also headed inland, pushing carts that were crammed with their belongings.

At camp, Gilbert, now understanding Japanese quite well, heard one of the guards remark to his companions that ever since our arrival there had been nothing but trouble. Now our not being wanted at the furnaces was just the latest thing that bothered them. Also, since we had come, camp routine had been shot to hell—it had gone smoothly before. Oddly, the group of guards blamed it all on us instead of the attacking American bombers. We learned that Lt. Kudeire, the camp commander, shared this strange viewpoint—Mitsui madness in Hidatchi.

Three blasts at 12:30 that afternoon did not stop the guards from sending us out to work at 1 P.M., even though no All Clear had sounded. Our job was to cut down trees on the wooded hill behind the barracks and slide the logs down to the camp for construction of a stronger air-raid shelter.

We had reached the top after a hard climb and were catching our breath when the expected raid took place. We had a ringside seat overlooking Hidatchi. Six Navy pursuit planes swooped down and fired their guns and rockets on what was left of the ruined city. I clearly saw one plane fire a rocket from each wing and drop a small bomb. The show ended with a single B-29 flying over, taking pictures of the results. On the horizon, we could barely distinguish a fleet of warships steaming southward toward Tokyo.

After the raid we threw a few logs down the hill and soon returned to the camp ourselves. We found the barracks had been strafed a bit—a .50 caliber projectile had lodged in the backboard of Frank Garcia's bunk. Frank's bunk was next to mine, and I helped him dig out the shell.

The men who had stayed in camp had been ordered to lie down on the floor inside the barracks during the raid. None were injured, but outside the building the pursuit planes had wrecked two trucks loaded with rice. The raid had also cut the overhead power lines serving the barracks, leaving us without electricity. All Clear had not yet sounded by the time we had finished our normal supper of white rice and soup.

The next day, July 19, 1945, we started digging a tunnel into the hillside in back of the barracks. It could be a very good air-raid shelter, but would it be finished in time? After thinking more about a landing, I now hoped our boys wouldn't do it. If they did, our forces would prepare the way by shelling and burning this whole valley and coastline to ashes. It would be suicide to be within 20 miles of Hidatchi. But everything was quiet during the day—a good sign. Thank God!

Yet at 11:30 P.M. three blasts signaled another raid. Five minutes later, planes began dropping incendiaries on Hidatchi and along the coast. Because of the overcast, I couldn't make out for sure what kind of aircraft they were but believe they were B-25s. There seemed to be only 25 or so of them, but they did a lot of damage—hits on gas storage tanks caused large explosions. Again no antiaircraft fire or fighter planes challenged the bombers.

The raid lasted about an hour, but there was no All Clear signal, so I finally went to bed an hour after the raid ended. During 7 A.M. roll call, a photo plane flew over Hidatchi and then flew away to the south, dropping a few bombs over the next ridge. There were no work details so I contentedly slept all morning after being up for so long during the night.

The previous night our guards had been called out to restrain some Koreans who had broken into a nearby warehouse to steal some rice and vegetables. The guards had to do a lot more shoving and shouting than before to control these Koreans, who used to be sneaky rather than bold.

Perhaps shaky from the encounter with the Koreans, one guard came up to me this afternoon and asked, "Were the raids at Kawasaki the same as here?" I replied, "Yes, but a lot worse." Then he asked, "Are we safe where we are?" When I told him we were in a fairly safe location, he thanked me and ran off to tell his equally-frightened friends. Even though the Japanese do not show fear in their faces, they could feel fear. I felt sorry for the guards, as well as the countless civilian refugees who had pushed their carts of belongings past our camp to get away from Hidatchi. It was a prime target because of its electrical power production. The heavy attacks had made many refugees out of its population of 250,000. Factory people who had stayed were put on two-thirds' rations because the factory had no work for them, although it kept feeding them.

On July 21 the General Alarm blew twice during the night. I got up, dressed, and stood by; but the three blasts for an actual raid did not follow, so I lost a lot of sleep for nothing. Yet we had so many fleas that nobody could sleep well anyway. The next morning Garcia and I shook out our mats, but we weren't too sure it would help in our open sleeping quarters. Yet I woke up the following morning after a good, mostly free-of-fleas sleep.

I felt so good I volunteered to work on the air-raid shelter. Lunch consisted of seaweed soup that tasted good to me but not to many others, so I had my fill of it. I intended to rebuild this skinny body so I could live through this situation and return home on my own two feet. In the beautiful afternoon I sat in the sun and read the Personal Memoir of U.S. Grant, an interesting book—I learned later that Grant's work is considered one of the greatest military memoirs of world history, ranking with those of Julius Caesar and Napoleon.

The same afternoon Lt. Kudeire left for Tokyo to find out what to do with us since the furnaces had shut down. Apparently communications and transportation between here and Tokyo had been cut off by air raids, so he might be gone for a few days. Meantime, Kudeire's staff assigned almost everyone to cleaning up the rubble of homes and factories in Hidatchi. I volunteered to stay in camp with a few men to work on the air-raid shelter. When the detail came back from Hidatchi, they reported finding an unexploded shell that measured 16 inches across—meaning that a battleship had been shelling Hidatchi rather than a cruiser, which fired smaller shells.

The next day, on July 25, Lt. Kudeire returned from Tokyo with instructions for us to go back to the furnaces. But the next morning the furnace boss still didn't have much for us to do. After lunch we were about to head back to the furnaces anyway when Kudeire suddenly turned us around and sent us down to Hidatchi with the other two shifts—so much for his orders from Tokyo to support the furnaces.

In Hidatchi we stopped at a burnt-out warehouse that was full of salt, parched beans, still-hot rice, and barley. The boys who had gone down in the morning told our shift about the warehouse, so I brought along a pillow slip. I filled it with table salt and stuffed myself with parched beans while we sacked and loaded the hot rice, beans, and barley on the camp truck. Back at camp we spread the hot rice on a cement floor to dry and cool. There was no shakedown, so everyone's pockets were bulging with grain or salt as we entered the barracks. I could barely eat supper because I'd eaten so many beans—my appetite finally sated. At 10:30 P.M. three blasts got us out of bed, but nothing happened so we went to sleep. The next morning, while helping to arrange all the loot in our storeroom, my appetite was back to normal, so I stuffed myself with slightly-burned raw rice—it had a good flavor. Yet we had to take the sacks of rice we had stored back out to the main gate a few days later during an alert because the guards figured the camp buildings were in danger.

The day we filled the storeroom a single B-29 flew over and interrupted our work at camp before vanishing to the north. We had forgotten about the bomber and gone back to work when suddenly we heard bombs whistling down on the city below us—we were glad we had emptied the warehouse yesterday rather than this morning. It was the B-29 which had circled back to drop "eggs" on some target that the flyboys had missed on previous raids. The bomber made just one run and then continued toward Tokyo. But there was a scary ending to that small raid. Our boys who were down in Hidatchi that morning were working very close to the only untouched building in the factory area when the bombs came down. One bomb hit the center of the building—obliterating it and throwing some of our boys who were near the building two or three feet in the air. But none of them were hurt except for minor scratches.

On July 29 they sent us up to the furnaces again. We had just started work when the General Alarm blew, but now they let us take cover away from the furnaces. During one of the numerous alerts that day I started talking with a Japanese furnace boss who spoke some English. But our friendly conversation turned sour when he asked, "Do you like Japan and the Japanese people?" I had not worried about somewhat sharp discussions with civilian bosses at Kawasaki, so I answered the question with an emphatic "No!" But this civilian translated our conversation to a guard sitting near us with his rifle and bayonet across his knee. He jumped to his feet and thrust his sharp bayonet a few inches from my stomach and held it there. I stared back at him as we stood motionless and speechless for a few seconds before he drew back and sat down.

About August 1 our work detail, which was assigned to cleaning up the rubble in Hidatchi, was made permanent. It was not hard work, but we had to walk an hour to reach the ruined city. Since the area was all burned out, there was no danger of bombing. At camp I was a member of the "demolition squad" that was supposed to defuse any bombs that were close by and didn't explode. I was chosen because of my job of loading bombs at Clark Field. Now my knowledge of bombs exposed me to more danger because I had to stay close to the camp buildings during raids, as well as defusing any unexploded bombs.

On August 2 a report reached us that Kawasaki had been leveled by our bombers, and our Mitsui Camp No. 2 was blown to pieces—resulting in many prisoner casualties.* The Steel Mill camp also suffered many casualties. This news made me see red—the Japs had sacrificed some of my very best friends because they would not move them out of the target area. But God must have been watching over me, since I had already been moved out of there. Of course, the war was not over yet, but from then on I felt certain I would make it. Yet the destruction of Kawasaki made me worry that my mother and family would no longer believe I was still alive—not knowing of my move to Hidatchi.

About this time I made friends with Brontz, a young Dutchman who had been brought up in Java, a Dutch colony. He wanted to learn

---

*The Mitsui Madhouse was destroyed by an American raid on July 25—twenty-three days after our departure. But all except the fire party had evacuated to shelters and were safe. The 22 fire-fighters who were killed included Lt. Carney. After the war, Doc Curtin reported that Carney had been mainly responsible for getting the secure shelters constructed that had saved most of the prisoners.

how to speak English so I agreed to help him; he was an apt student but stumbled on pronunciation. We also got together on trading food. Like other Dutch, Brontz liked bread better than rice because it could be set aside to be eaten later—unlike cooked rice. But there was always the chance of it spoiling too soon if the weather was hot and damp.

On August 6 a group of us watched the coolies trying to light up the furnaces, but they could only get one going. Then we couldn't do any work because of numerous air alerts. The next day at the furnace, during another alert, I climbed over a ridge and found myself alone in a grove of cherry trees—some still in bloom. One B-29 flew over, and then everything was still. I lay down on the grass and looked upward at the pink blossoms and the vivid blue sky. I forgot the hated word "war" and our lowly state as prisoners of war. A feeling of being near God swept over me, and I fell into a restful sleep for an hour or so. Then I roamed among the trees, eating the occasional cherry that had ripened until the All Clear signal called me back to virtual slavery.

I learned later that, oddly enough, I was enjoying nature's beauty at almost the same time that the war took a final, decisive turn—at 8:15 that morning a B-29 dropped an atomic bomb on Hiroshima. But looking back, I could see no noticeable difference in our treatment afterwards—I doubt that the camp commander and guards knew anything about Hiroshima for some time because of censorship.

On August 7 an alert woke us up at 1 A.M. I hurried outside with my evacuation bag, but the All Clear signal sent us back to bed a half-hour later. After breakfast that morning, we could see it was going to he hot, but I felt all right and didn't mind joining the ten-man garden detail. We expected to work at one of the gardens close to the camp, but the guards marched us down to the outskirts of Hidatchi. We soon found that we were to clear brush and rocks away from a patch of ground that was to be a new camp garden—heavy work on a day that had become very hot. It wasn't long before perspiration was pouring from us. I was wielding a hoe when I suddenly found myself falling—I ended up on my knees, trying to figure out why I had fallen.

The Jap guard made me sit in the shade with my head between my knees until my head quit spinning. I was still resting at 10:30 A.M. when an alert sounded and we headed back to the camp. Dr. Kaufman had me stay in for the afternoon. I slept until 4 P.M. and then helped the cooks clean some burnt rice.

That night after roll call, Captain DeJager, our Dutch senior officer, called all the NCOs to his office. He wanted us NCOs to settle the numerous petty arguments that flared up between the enlisted Javanese boys before they became serious. There was little discussion, but none of us was against doing what he could to help.

On August 8 I went out to work with two swell Norwegians, Christiansen and Jacobsen. They had been taken off a merchant ship in the North Sea by the Germans, who had then dropped them off in Japan. They had learned to speak English by being with the British prisoners at another camp, so the Norwegians spoke with a "limey" accent. Otherwise they seemed like typical Yanks.

Christensen was nicknamed the "Shadow" because he was quick and quiet in movement. He used this skill in a continuous contest with the Japs to steal as much as he could—whether he needed the loot or not. As a result, he had a small grocery store under his bunk. He easily got me interested in his thievery, so that one day we prowled through a dark factory but found nothing of interest. But Christiansen's physique did not quite match his nickname—he was large and powerfully built, and could outwork any of us but seldom exerted himself.

That night we had entrail soup, but it tasted good. After dark I looked up at the stars, which filled the black, cloudless sky from horizon to horizon—a beautiful night and perfect for dropping bombs all over Japan.

The next day I was at the furnace again with the two Norwegians. Each of us had some raw rice to cook. But to do so was strictly forbidden. Our solution was for one of us to cook while the others distracted the guard with dumb questions.

We worked again that night because the three of us volunteered for the night shift, which started at 10 P.M. We believed that shift offered better opportunities for stealing, cooking rice, and napping. When Jacobsen awoke me at 9:15 P.M. for the new shift, I found that the camp and entire valley was blacked out. Then the men we relieved told us the Japs were very nervous because they expected a shelling from the U.S. Navy.

Yet the boss did not seem nervous as he piled work on me. I didn't even have a chance to sit down while I was there—so much for the idea of the night shift being a good deal. I wasn't saved until the alarm blew at 4:30 A.M. Then we headed for our new air-raid tunnel in back of the camp. We were stuck there until All Clear sounded four hours later. There was no space to lie down, so I was very uncomfortable, being tired and sore after a long night of work. But at least we felt safe.

I was still catching up on my sleep when Walter Kritzon awoke me at 2 P.M. to report that an alarm had just sounded. Still dopey from heavy sleeping, I heard muffled explosions and saw flashes in the sky—apparently a large raid was going on. But a moment later I changed my mind when lightening struck near us with an overwhelming burst of thunder, triggering the heaviest rain I had ever seen.

I watched the storm for a short time and then went back to sleep. When I awoke refreshed later in the afternoon, everyone was talking excitedly about the news that Russia had declared war on Japan and was moving into Manchuria. I thought Russia might be cashing in on an Allied victory that was about to happen—thus gaining slices of Korea and Manchuria. Also, Russia could be planning to participate in the final invasion of Japan. I fervently hoped that was not the case, because we still believed what our guards at Kawasaki had told us—that we would be executed in case of an invasion of Japan so that our Jap guards could join the fight against the landing forces. But how could the war end without an invasion—the Japs were too stupid to surrender, even though their principal cities had been devastated. Then my mind grappled with the unhappy thought that now the Russians would join the Americans in bombing, strafing, and shelling us.

As a staff sergeant, I was the highest rated noncom on our night shift, so the Japs chose me to be shift boss for the night of August 12 and 13 when the elderly Jap civilian boss was not available for some reason. I chose Private Walter Kritzon as my assistant. After we got all the men working, Kritzon and I brewed and then ate rice in continuing cycles until 2 A.M. Then we gathered some hot blocks from the furnace to provide hot water for the men to bathe themselves after work. But when an alarm stopped work at 4:45 A.M., we led the men into the tunnel—just before a flight of carrier planes began to strafe the furnaces and whole factory area.

The raid lasted an hour or more. But even when it seemed to be over we stayed in the shelter quite a bit longer while the Jap foreman repeatedly complained, "Hurry up and get back to work." But I just ignored him. He could not force us back to work by himself—he needed a camp guard to overrule me, and none was around. I finally released the shift for work, although the All Clear still had not sounded. In the early daylight, the buildings looked like sieves where they had been riddled with machine gun fire. The Japs were amazed when I showed them a piece of railroad track with a clean hole in it—a .50 caliber armor-piercing shell had gone clear through. Our relief finally arrived at 8:30 A.M.—two and a half hours late. Then our boys finally took their baths before going back to camp.

All the morning of August 13, Army P-51s, carrier planes, and heavy bombers flew southward above heavy clouds. They kept me awake, even though I was pretty tired after a long night of cooking and eating rice and listening to the complaints of the Japanese foreman about us not leaving the air-raid shelter. But I couldn't get to sleep in the barracks, so in the afternoon I took a blanket out by the back gate and lay down under some trees. Then at 1:30 P.M., and again at 5 P.M., large flights of heavy bombers flew over—noisy but invisible above the low-hanging clouds. After All Clear at 6:15 P.M., I still wanted to sleep and did so until our night shift.

Then I had an easy shift, except for having a lot of trouble keeping away from a pro–Jap Javanese. He kept helping the Jap civilian boss find me—the boss was yelling my number whenever he wanted anything, while I was trying to stay out of sight.

XIX

Peace

August 15, 1945, to September 8, 1945

On August 15 there was little work for our afternoon shift, and we did nothing. Only one-third of Oven number 5 was burning, while Oven number 1 had only enough fire to keep the ore from hardening and forming blocks that would have to be chipped out. The Japs didn't bother to yell at us but just sat around in small groups talking quietly. Did that mean what I hoped?

Taking advantage of the Japs' inattention, Jacobsen and I slipped away to look in the window of a factory office. An open safe stood in the corner, but, more fascinating, a stack of rectangular shapes that looked like gold ingots lay on the floor by the safe. We thought we could break into the office easily, but there were so many coolies around that we decided to wait until the next night. Once we stole one or two bars, we could figure out how to get the treasure back to the States.

Putting off the break-in, Jacobsen and I returned to camp with our shift. There the astounding news greeted us that the war was over. My God! I hoped this news was true! But something had to be going on because Cpl. Oto hurriedly left for Tokyo. Just before dark that evening, Jacobsen and I headed for the factory office as we had planned. Nobody was around to stop us from getting in, but the safe was closed and the gold had vanished, so what was the use of breaking the door down?

There were no work details that night nor air activity. Another good sign—civilians were dragging carts with their belongings past the camp, returning to Hidatchi from the mountains. The guards were glued to the newspaper, but we didn't know exactly what was happening. Yet the next night shift, on August 17, was supposed to go to work, and my shift was scheduled for that afternoon. Then these work details were canceled by instructions from Tokyo brought back by Cpl. Oto late on August 16. The next morning Lt. Kudeire, the Camp Commander, left with his luggage, leaving Cpl. Oto in charge.

At 7 A.M. that day Captain DeJager called all the prisoner NCOs to his office. He told us that the Allies and Japan were holding a fifteen-day conference to discuss peace procedures. In the meantime, we were not to go out on work details except for wood, vegetables, and routine camp tasks. Camp requirements for us would stay the same—such as saluting and roll call. DeJager said he would get for us as many cigarettes and as much soap as he could. At 8:30 he made the same announcement to the men downstairs, and Lt. Aanderviel made the announcement to the Javanese upstairs. Now I was sure the war was over! The story of the fifteen-day conference was just a way to maintain order in the camp.

Now the news of peace was the only topic of conversation, but there was no shouting and yelling, as might have been expected. For myself, the full import of being able to look far into the future as a free man just hadn't sunk in. We were so used to living from day to day that it was difficult to grasp the idea of planning ahead for a new life. Ed Lubiewski and I spent all morning talking about what it would be like being back in the States, but the main thing we discussed was the good food we were going to eat.

That afternoon the barracks became uncomfortably warm. It was a hot day, and the building was filled with our men, who no longer were going on work details. I went out to nap under our one cherry tree. Before I fell asleep, four Japanese pursuit planes flew over, heading south—presumably to be turned over to the Allied forces.

The next day, after another nap under the cherry tree, I won a lot of soap in a raffle of Red Cross items—we couldn't get any soap our first winter at Kawasaki. Good luck continued when my friend Walter Kritzon gave me a Red Cross razor he had won. I hadn't had a razor for a year—since I had broken the one my mother had sent. But with nothing to do, time was beginning to weigh on our hands. Yet, along with boredom, peace brought changes for the better. We were allowed to sleep on the roof, away from the fleas and the hot interior of the barracks, which trapped and held the day's heat during August. And the guards raffled off a lot of Red Cross clothing that they had neglected to distribute in the past two years. Although I didn't win any clothing, I did partake fully in our richer diet. The galley roasted a pig, baked bread, and gave us lots of barley—so much barley that I became literally sick of it and gave some of it away to

Ed Lubiewski. My weight was up to 150 pounds from a low of 124 when rations were really short.

By August 20 everyone had become very restless and anxious for something to happen. We were waiting that day for the camp commander to return—he was expected to have orders for us to move. But he didn't show up until 4:30 the next morning, when I woke up on the roof to see him coming in the front gate. At 10:30 we eagerly assembled to learn from Captain DeJager what Lt. Kudeire had told him. But we found that we were just to wait until the Allies came for us, and Lt. Kudeire didn't say when that would be. There were no happy faces among us.

That afternoon we NCOs went to Captain DeJager's office to complain about the four-fifths ration that the Japs were giving us—a vestige of the ration for the sick during the war because the ill men didn't go and work in the factories. Now we argued that there should be no reduction in rations at all since the war was over. We also wanted to have one of us NCOs act as the American representative to have a say in Captain DeJager's decisions—he was Dutch.

DeJager accepted S/Sgt. John Seres as our representative after M/Sgts. Oricht and Nettles refused the responsibility. DeJager also said he would try to secure full rations for us. We convinced him that work in the camp garden would be worthless to us, since we would be leaving soon. While I was at the meeting, Ed cooked up enough of my hoard of rice to provide a full ration for himself, Walter Kritzon, Christiansen, and me. A few days later, our session with Captain DeJager seemed to have paid off, because Seres was able to have us put on full rations, plus burnt rice.

Although I was not lucky in the recent clothes raffles, my friends fixed me up. Christiansen insisted that I take a new British woolen shirt, since he already had two shirts—Chris the Shadow seemed to have a good supply of everything. Then Mailloux gave me a pair of U.S. Marine Corps trousers, which had lots of lice eggs in the seams and a small hole in the seat. But Kritzon sewed a patch in the seat and I carefully scraped off the lice eggs. The result was a fine pair of pants that fit perfectly.

A day later we were to turn in excess clothing at the storeroom, but most of the men just tossed their old clothes over the fence to the Koreans. These workers were not POWs but had been conscripted—Korea was then a Japanese colony. I would have also given them my extra clothes if I had not been afraid the Koreans would get into trouble with the Japs by being conspicuous in wearing them. The Allied victory might not help these Koreans right away.

First thing on August 24 the Japs reported to us that the U.S. Air Corps would put on a large air show over Tokyo the next day. Afterwards, aircraft were to start dropping supplies to the Prisoner of War (PW) camps in the area. Captain DeJager announced that all supplies dropped for our camp would be turned in to his office for distribution. Then he selected a detail to collect wood, wire and paint for constructing a PW sign that could be seen by the American aircraft. But the officers couldn't agree on the size of the PW sign—they bickered until 11 A.M. Then we formed and painted a large, yellow PW sign on black background in the camp assembly area.

But we believed it would be a few days before anything could be dropped, because our valley was socked in with fog, making it too dangerous for aircraft to fly low enough for a successful drop. The next morning the fog lifted briefly, but in the afternoon the sky clouded over and it began to rain. The ceiling was still too low the next day. Oddly, there were alarms sounded that day and the next—some Japs must still be nervous, or they hadn't received the word. With nothing to do, I was getting out of shape, so I did some mild calisthenics.

On August 26 Captain DeJager told us that Lt. Kudeire had heard over the radio that the Allies had landed in Tokyo at midnight. Cpl. Oto told us that aircraft had dropped supplies on other prison camps that morning. But the upper end of our valley was still closed in.

The same day three of us senior NCOs met with Captain DeJager and Lt. Aanderviel about chow. There was a lot of white rice in the storeroom that we weren't using very fast. We wanted to make sure we ate most of it before we left. DeJager feared that we might use it up before we could get away. But we NCOs and Lt. Aanderviel overruled the conservative Captain. As a result, we were to have white rice twice a day at a rate that would use it all up in ten days. Lt. Aanderviel was to have the keys to the storeroom and oversee the issue of rice.

When I woke up on August 27, the ceiling had lifted. At 6:30 three gull-winged Corsairs flew over very low. One dropped a bag of cigarettes. As they headed back to their carriers, they dipped their wings—a friendly gesture, but when was anyone going to do anything about us? Then the boys found a note in the cigarette bag which said, "It will be just a few more days." Our spirits soared! Now they knew where we were, and there should be some action soon if the fog didn't sock us in again.

A couple of hours later a Corsair dropped a number of *Newsweek* magazines. I read a copy cover to cover—there was so much new information about the war that I didn't think I would ever get caught up on what had happened in the past three years all over the world. In the afternoon a dozen carrier planes came over to drop chocolate bars and cigarettes—the American Chesterfields and Lucky Strikes tasted like honey

F4U-4 Corsairs—three Navy, gull-winged Corsairs were the first to find our camp near Hidatchi—they flew low to cheer us up. (National Archives, 41641)

compared to the harsh Japanese cigarettes. The flyers purposely dropped the bags somewhat away from the camp to avoid hitting the half-wild, yelling men, of whom I was a part—as nuts with happiness as the rest. As the bags were still falling, some of the men would race out to get one. Sometimes a guard would try to make a race of it, but none could keep up with the fast Americans. What a wonderful sight—to see our own planes flying so low we could see the pilots waving their arms and dipping their wings in greeting!

Later that afternoon we learned the Army wanted us to volunteer to stay as part of the occupation of Japan—either as soldiers or civilians. The Army, anxious to organize for a long occupation, was trying to recruit us while we were still in PW camp. Since I was a noncom officer, I was offered a commission—with it would come authority and advantages. Even in prison camp the officers hadn't had to work. But I didn't even start to consider the idea of staying—I wanted to get home. Some of the noncoms did become officers in that way and thus were on hand to testify at the War Crimes Trials in Yokohama.

M/Sgt. John Britton stayed to testify—he was a good witness because of his POW job of assigning men to the different factory details. Our witnesses made possible the sentencing of Sgt. Shiozawa to 20 years of hard labor, Little Henry (Lt. Myazaki) to 40 years, and Bucktooth (Kasuya) to 20 years. But they were released in 1958 when a general amnesty took place. Kondo, our friendly interpreter, was not charged by us, but the British charged him for behavior at their camp before he came to ours. However, he got off with one year. Appendix B lists some members of the Japanese staff at Kawasaki who were convicted, and their sentences.

A single gull-wing plane flew over during breakfast, and since it was a beautiful day, I expected a lot of drops. Waiting for the excitement, I took off my shirt and lay down to sunbathe on the roof—a good place to view the show. Sure enough, about 8:30 six gull-wing jobs buzzed the camp and dropped three sea bags crammed with soap, cigarettes, magazines, chocolate bars, and canned food. Some of the cans broke, so we gave them to the galley to put in our soup. One bag had a note that asked us what we wanted most—we spelled out on the ground News and Food. After the next flight we had so much food that Captain DeJager's office became stacked like a supermarket. The payoff of the food drops came at 3 P.M. when we had a lunch of fried beefsteak, fried potatoes, corn on the cob, and ham and flour soup.

At the same time Lt. Aanderviel took charge of the storeroom, Captain DeJager replaced Lt. Kudeire as Camp Commander—a change so quiet that I knew nothing of it until it was all over. That night I became so full that I had to give my rice away or I would have become sick. Before dark we took some white sheets and printed on them 350 THANKS and stretched them on the ground across the river where the Yank flyers could see them the next time they came. The next day the bounty continued when twelve Corsairs dropped ten cases of clothing, cigarettes, food, and magazines. There were enough K-rations to provide four boxes for each five men—they surely tasted good.

By August 29 the boys were scattering candy wrappers, empty cans, and K-ration boxes all over the place. Staff/Sgt. John Seres, who had taken the top NCO responsibility under Captain DeJager, noticed the mess. He asked Lockerman, a Dutchman from Java, and me to form a detail and clean up the camp. We rounded up some men, and they had the camp looking shipshape in an hour.

Later in the morning a lone B-29 flew over slowly and made a perfect hit on a field near us.* So many 55-gallon drums came tumbling out

---

*B-29s dropped supplies on 154 POW camps in August and September 1945. Birdsall, Saga of the Flying Fortress, page 314.

of the plane that I thought they would never stop. It was a stunning sight, but the drums were dropped so low that the chutes didn't have time to open, causing a lot of the canned stuff to be broken or badly dented. We didn't care, however, because most of it could be used by the galley. In the middle of the afternoon the mess crew served us split pea soup with potatoes in it, and then for supper we had white rice, potato salad, chicken noodle soup, and fruit salad. I was fool enough to accept an extra rice ration, but I couldn't eat it. The other senior NCOs and I met with Captain DeJager about questions of camp life. We decided to have a clothes issue tomorrow, since we had a supply from all the drops.

The next morning I felt fine except for being half-sick from the rich food I had eaten the day before. Just before lunch I was lying in my favorite spot on the porch roof when some carrier planes came over and played around. Some of the Java boys scrambled out of a window onto the roof to see better. In their excitement they jumped up and down so hard that the whole darn roof collapsed. It was about ten feet to the ground and we were all badly bruised, but no one was seriously hurt. I was so damn mad I almost killed one of the Javanese before I saw the humor of the situation and let him go. I was particularly put out because my glasses were twisted out of shape, but Lt. Aanderviel fixed them for me with a soldering iron.

The next day I was still very sore from the fall, so I let Lockerman take the daily cleanup detail while I stayed in bed. The Java boys who brought the roof down came to see me and were so apologetic that I felt sorry I had blown up and grabbed one of them yesterday. But there was still some resentment inside me. Later in the day, after the Dutch doctor looked at my bruises, he advised me in a light tone, "Take it easy. You'll probably survive." That made me mad, and I came back with, "You're damn right I'll survive, but I know some boys who'll never see Java again if they break down the roof again." The doctor just gave me a wry grin. I soon regretted saying that—even though he was Dutch and responsible for the Javanese in a sense, he couldn't stop that little accident from happening.

I guess I was just jumpy from the excitement of the last few days— being over-anxious to get back to the old U.S.A. The good food was affecting everyone—tempers were getting short, and the main topic of conversation changed from food to what type of woman each man liked as a bed partner. I hadn't even thought of women as objects of sexual desire, apparently because I just hadn't had enough meat for sex (or the lack of it) to bother me.

The next day, September 1, all Americans turned in unworn Red

Cross clothing for new GI khaki trousers, shirts, and Army field jackets. It felt wonderful to wear clean clothes that fit—the planes had dropped a number of sizes. But an interpreter told us that one "supply" B-29 had crashed into a mountain. The new Japanese lieutenant said that, starting tonight, we should be ready to leave for Yokohama at a moment's notice. He said we should be out of there at least by the Tenth of September.

After supper the next day, September 2, the Japanese guards turned in their rifles and were given armbands. They were now classified as MPs, since the Japanese Army no longer existed. That was the immediate result of the surrender terms between Japan and the Allies, which had been signed that morning aboard the Battleship Missouri in Tokyo Bay.

We started hiking details yesterday for the exercise and to look around. But I still chose to stay in camp because my heel was still healing. After lunch, eight younger and exceptionally restless Americans just plain took off for Tokyo. Nobody knew of the disappearance until hours later. We were not supposed to go wandering around the countryside without authority and a Japanese MP to protect us from any bitter civilians.

Captain DeJager sent Sergeants Hoy and Brock out to bring the boys back. But after waiting for a couple of hours, DeJager had to report the missing men to the Japanese Lieutenant—the Japanese had the responsibility of turning over all of us to American authorities. Next, DeJager held a roll call to see if any more of us were missing.

Then after Hoy and Brock had still not come back, Sgt. John Seres asked me, "Herb, would you like to go out with Captain DeJager, the new Japanese officer, and me to hunt for the whole bunch?" I didn't want to go off in a hostile country on a futile search, but said, "I just don't think I would be of much help. Maybe someone who knew a little Japanese would be a better choice." Before long the search party left—it had added Sgt. Wallie Henson, who apparently went in my place.

The departure left the camp in a buzz of discussion. We didn't settle down until midnight when the search party returned with Hoy and Brock and three of the original escapees. The searchers had found Hoy and Brock trying to talk three of the runaways into coming back to camp. All eight of them had been found together, but five wouldn't stop to listen to arguments for returning—such as the danger of traveling alone in an enemy county that had been recently devastated by American bombers. The impatience of the eight young men was understandable, but we older men didn't think they showed much discipline or concern for their own safety.

At breakfast on September 4 we received word we were to leave camp the next day at 7 A.M. Then I saw Armstrong and Hough head downstairs. But I didn't realize what was going on until everyone else made a mad rush for the stairs. We had waited for a long time for the husky Armstrong to get even with Hough, who had beaten him unmercifully at the Kawasaki camp. At that time Armstrong had been caught stealing rice, and the Japanese guards had ordered Hough to punish Armstrong by striking him repeatedly. Hough had not held back his punishing blows and had beaten Armstrong to a pulp. In contrast, when others of us had been ordered to beat a fellow prisoner, we had been able to look like we were striking the victim harder than we were—we satisfied the guards without badly hurting the prisoner being punished.

Now Armstrong probably figured that this last day in prison camp would be the best time for him to get back at Hough—the Japanese were not in control of the camp, and we were not yet under American military administration (then a serious fight would not be tolerated). It was almost over before I could push my way through the crowd to see. Hough was already lying on the ground, bleeding from the face, while Armstrong was kicking him. When some of the boys yelled at him to stop, Armstrong growled, "What the hell! He did the same thing to me three years ago!" Then three men grabbed the powerful Marine. Otherwise, Armstrong would have killed him. Now Donald Mailloux, Hough's closest friend, helped him to the hospital section. The doctor sewed three stitches across a deep cut under Hough's left eye. Nothing could be done about the teeth that were knocked out. When Hough limped back to the barracks, nobody paid any attention to him. Back at Kawasaki, Hough had disfigured Armstrong and probably adversely affected Armstrong's health for life. But instead of thinking about Hough and Armstrong, everyone was excited about leaving camp the next morning.

September 5 started early with reveille at 4 A.M., followed by a breakfast of fried squash, thick squash, and black bean soup, which all tasted good to me. Then the busy galley gave us each a loaf of barley bread to take along for lunch. At 6 A.M., as we fell in with all our gear, somebody noticed a movement far up the narrow mountain road we had taken so often to our furnace details. We all kept looking and soon could make out a column of men marching in our direction. As they came closer we saw a large American flag being carried in front of the column that was strung out along the narrow road. Father back, a British flag became visible, and then a Dutch flag waved above the middle of the long column. The marchers moved toward us at a steady pace with flags flying proudly and then turned into our compound. The newcomers were 65 Americans, 141 Dutch and Javanese, and, oddly, 80 Chinese who marched in under the

British flag. They had all been held farther up the mountain at the "Yamamoto" camp. All groups from both camps now mingled in a constant jabbering exchange of war stories that lasted the best part of an hour. We learned that the newcomers had constructed the flags by cutting and dying pieces of silk from the parachutes that had dropped supplies for them. The Chinese prisoners had some connection with the Royal Air Force so had constructed the British flag.

At 7 A.M. we formed a new, longer column, with Americans gathering behind the American flag, the Chinese behind their British flag, and the Dutch and Javanese behind the Dutch flag. I was glad to have American officers in charge again, although Captain DeJager, our Dutch camp commander, had done a good job after the Japanese commander gave up control. As we marched to the Hidatchi railroad station, we were seeing the last of the camp Japanese; a few of the guards, who had become MPs, walked along on both sides of the long column to protect us from the supposedly hostile populace—they said nothing to us and little among themselves, looking a little out of place and probably feeling not needed.

As we marched, I had a strange feeling about leaving a way of life that was so familiar—I must be in a dream that would vanish when I woke up. Others must have had similar imaginings because we said very little until we boarded the train and headed north. Then it came home to us that our new life was real—our conversation became hot and heavy about going home, seeing family and friends, and enjoying better food and sleeping conditions right away.

Time flew on our two-hour ride along Japan's east coast. The train drew up by a pier at the small fishing village of Onhoma, which was close to the city of Sendai. We climbed off and stood by the water, waiting for something to happen—nobody was there to meet us. We had been noticed, however, because two Navy Corsairs soon buzzed us and then disappeared. But they had dropped a note that told us that we hadn't been expected until the next day. It seemed that there had been orders for us to delay one day, but they had not reached either of our two camps.

But before dark we were settled in a large, empty schoolhouse in the center of town. It was clean and dry, but there was no place to sleep except the floor. So much for the new, comfortable life we had talked about on the train. But our food wasn't so bad. It came from a Canadian camp ten miles away—their galley sent in all the rice we could eat, plus two cans of Campbell's green pea soup for each man. The supply aircraft must have dropped too much pea soup for the Canadians. I ate one can of soup cold and found it delicious.

After dark, Mailloux and I were so restless we walked about the sleeping town for a couple of hours before turning in. But some of the healthier men had traded soap, cigarettes, and chewing gum to some of the local girls and were sleeping with them. Oh well, that was more comfortable than the hard, wooden floor of the school building. The next morning five men were missing at roll call, but they soon came up the street, each bringing a giggling Japanese girl to show where he had been. The girls looked neat and clean—maybe they had used the soap they had gained.

After sleeping more in the morning, I walked all over town, looking for a drink of sake, but there was none to be had—I wanted to see what it was like.

The Canadian camp had no more food to give us, so we had only plain rice. But that evening Sgt. Charles Johnson and I were invited into a Japanese home for tea with pickled onions and cucumber. I felt guilty eating their food, because they had so little for themselves. I carried the brunt of the conversation because Johnson spoke no Japanese. I tried to explain about all the food, clothing, radios, and automobiles in most homes in America. They seemed amazed, but I don't think they believed all I was saying. Having lived at the same level as these poor, starved people for so long, it was even hard for me to realize that a more comfortable life lay ahead of me.

This tired old man and his obedient wife used words that I could not understand, but I could tell what they wanted me to know. They were sorry that we had to suffer as prisoners of their people, and that the Japanese people did not desire the war. They put these thoughts in so many ways that I was sure they were sincere. I believed they spoke for the many simple, down-trodden people of Japan. I should hate the Japanese people, but could only feel the deepest sympathy for them. While my life was about to start anew, theirs was to be a hard struggle to regain the little they once had. Why must so many suffer for the greed and ambition of so few?

The next day, September 7, we were still in our makeshift situation—sleeping in the large schoolhouse and eating plain rice three times a day. A group of us walked around town and the surrounding countryside that morning, but my feet got so sore that I slept all afternoon. Our ranking officer, Captain Underwood of the 31st Infantry Division, went to Yokohama the previous day to obtain orders for us, but he hadn't returned yet. He was rumored to have been General MacArthur's chauffeur in Manila—if that were true, Underwood should be able to get us out of here soon.

Many of us were getting restless again and talking about taking off for Yokohama—this time I might have joined. But a Radio Tokyo broadcast told all ex-prisoners to be patient and wait where we were until brought to Yokohama. At 6 P.M., however, Captain Underwood returned with lots of K-rations—three per man and, more important, news that we were to leave for Yokohama in the morning.

Nobody missed roll call at 4:30 A.M. the next day. At 5:30 a long journey began by streetcar and dusty train to Shinagawa. There we boarded a clean, fast electric train that sped us to Yokohama. As we got off the train, the 1st Cavalry Division (Airborne) band played a rousing "Hail, Hail, the Gang's All Here." Then soldiers of the U.S. Army, ranging from three-star generals to privates, ran up to us and greeted us like long-lost brothers. I couldn't even come up with a cheerful "hello" because I was choked up and on the verge of tears. But I didn't feel so foolish when I noticed that my buddies were also having a hard time answering this wonderful welcome.

As we walked toward the end of the station platform, the first American woman I had seen in three years grabbed my attention—she was an Army nurse and so beautiful I couldn't take my eyes off her. She noticed my interest; when we came face to face, she gave me a big smile and said, "Welcome home, soldier!" I almost passed out but was able to pause and chat with her for a few moments before we were hustled down the platform to waiting trucks. We didn't even get to hold hands, but I fell in love with her and would have married her right then. Instead, I could only wave goodbye as our trucks pulled away.

A short ride of a few miles took us to our first American meal. I heaped my tray with the delicious food but could only eat a few spoonfuls of the rich servings. From habit, I picked up my tray and headed for the door—I would eat it all later. But a sergeant spotted me and gently took the tray, saying, "You're home now, soldier; there's lots more where that came from. Anytime you get a little hungry, come back and we'll fix you up." I felt like a big, dumb recruit, but at the same time joyfully realized I was back where people are treated like human beings—not like animals.

Thus I end my account of World War II service. The passage of over 50 years has made me more aware than ever of the countless blessings of freedom to which a citizen of the United States is entitled. May God strike me dead if I ever should forget to appreciate that freedom.

Epilogue

The day after our arrival in Yokohama, doctors gave us cursory physical examinations and divided us between those fit to make the trip to the U.S. by ship and those who should be flown directly to hospitals in the Philippines or Hawaii because of their rundown condition. My tests showed that I suffered from malnutrition, a bad case of hemorrhoids, and a peptic ulcer—pretty good shape for a POW, so I would go by ship. First, though, I and others in fairly good shape were to be flown from Tokyo to Clark Field on huge B-24 bombers being used as transport planes. I was on one of three such planes with POWs which took off and kept in formation, so I could watch one of the B-24s during the flight.

We were all on our way over the ocean when, to my horror, the bomb bay doors of the neighboring B-24 opened suddenly and three or four bodies tumbled out! Later I learned that one of the Javanese had tripped the bomb-release switch in the bomb bay. The B-24 did not slow down and the bomb doors were closed. It would have been impossible to find the bodies, and no attempt was made to look for them.

We arrived without further incident at Clark Field, which I had seen destroyed in the early hours of the war. Now the grass runways had been lengthened and paved over, and many new buildings replaced those destroyed by the Japanese attack on December 8, 1941. We got off the plane and proceeded directly to the large base hospital for more examinations. Then the Army redid our service records and gave each of us an increase in rank. I became a Technical Sergeant and sewed the stripes on my new khaki uniforms.

By this time I no longer felt the need to save the rich American food on my tray for later—I could eat plenty all at one sitting. I had a strong craving for chocolate of all kinds—it took almost six months before I got over my chocolate binge. The rich food put fat on my waist, and my ribs could no longer be seen. At the same time, my energy level rose—a great feeling! Furthermore, the unsightly wound on my left heel began to heal from the inside. Miraculously, the old skin fell away like an onion being peeled and was replaced by healthy tissue. Once again I was able to wear proper shoes on both feet. What a blessing!

On September 21, 1945, we boarded a transport ship and headed for the U.S.A. After settling in, the crew treated us like royalty. They thought of every need and would not let us do anything but eat and sleep. After a few days we reached Hawaii. But I didn't go ashore since I felt happy and secure on board and was content to just look at the beautiful island. After an overnight stay, we continued eastward. We learned that our first stop would be in Vancouver, Canada, to let off the number of Canadians on board. Then our ship would take us to Ft Lewis, Washington.

In a few days we eased into the beautiful, enclosed harbor of Vancouver, British Columbia, causing all hell to break loose! Ships of all sizes blew horns and whistles while we moved through the harbor to our docking berth. The noise of the welcome was deafening as the Canadian sailors and soldiers rushed down the gangplank into the arms of screaming friends and loved ones—a beautiful sight to behold!

Only a short trip took us to the dock at Ft. Lewis. Here there was no greeting party except the Red Cross, which sold us a doughnut and coffee for a nickel—not really a bargain in those days. A pretty sorry greeting, I thought.

The Army sent us to the local hospital in Tacoma, Washington, for more testing, which showed I had still more ailments, namely, spinal arthritis, an erratic heart beat, and hookworms. I almost gagged on the large, football-shaped pills I took to get rid of the hookworms. The pills tasted like gasoline, but the hookworms gave up and left my intestines forever after two doses.

At the Tacoma hospital we were assigned hospitals to use that would be convenient after we got home. Mine was the Madigan General Hospital in Galesburg, Illinois, not far from my mother's house in St. Louis. Then we boarded a hospital train for the journey across the west. I'd never heard of such a train. In each car the seats had been removed and beds installed lengthwise under a large window on both sides of the car. Thus I could lie in bed and enjoy the mountainous scenery as the train sped me homeward. The meals were brought to our bedsides. What a way to travel! As if we weren't getting enough attention, Red Cross ladies boarded the train at each stop to pass out fruit and soft drinks or hot coffee. These ladies made us forget all about our experience at Ft. Lewis, where the Red Cross had coffee to buy as we set foot in the U.S. for the first time in three years. Now our travel across the country was a wonderful treat that was completely unexpected.

In a few days we crossed the Mississippi River into Illinois, and before long I stepped off the train in Galesburg and into the arms of my beautiful, loving mother and her sister, Aunt Emma. It was over six years since I had seen them. What a blessing to be home again! After checking in at Madigan Hospital, I was put on recuperation leave until the first of the year—needed treatment could wait until after the Christmas holidays. During the enjoyable holidays I decided to reenlist for three years. As a result, I now had a total of six months' recuperative and reenlistment leave, plus two weeks at a hotel of my choice with two guests at government expense. I chose the Elms Hotel in Excelsior Springs in the Ozark Mountains of Missouri. My mother, aunt, and I thoroughly enjoyed the accommodations and scenery of the Ozarks.

We had hardly returned to St. Louis when a wire from the Madigan Hospital ordered me to report to the Biltmore Hospital in Coral Gables, Florida. There a surgeon operated on my hemorrhoids. The operation itself wasn't so bad, but when he pulled the stitches a few days later, the pain was so great I must have risen two feet off the bed!

While recuperating, my mother and two brothers took me on rides in the countryside to pass the time. Hoping to lift me out of the depression that had set in, they asked me to talk about my war experiences but had no luck. Still holding everything in, I finally told my mother that I had to travel somewhere—I could no longer stay in St. Louis. My mother then arranged for me to draw my own money from our joint checking account from wherever I might be. I could secure the money simply by sending a request by telegram that contained a certain code word. She understood my restlessness, but I knew she was very sad when I climbed on a Greyhound bus headed for New Orleans.

Without being specific and boring to the reader, I drank a lot at every place I stopped—from New Orleans to San Antonio, to Los Angeles, to San Francisco, and back to St. Louis. In my travels, I acquired a car, but thank God I had enough sense to let someone else drive when I was "liquored up." After my drinking binge, I had used up all the back pay I had accumulated as a POW for three years. I had also used up all my leave by the spring of 1946 when I reported for postwar duty at March Field in Riverside, California, with a new, tailor-made "Ike" jacket and $100 to my name. But my restlessness was gone.

I was now a technical sergeant—having been automatically promoted from staff sergeant after my release from Japanese prison camp. At March Field I took up my prewar specialty of armaments—now I worked on the fighter aircraft of the 1st Fighter Group. I did well and was promoted to master sergeant by the end of the year. I had the same job for two years, becoming quite proficient in the guns and their fire control on fighter aircraft. But as master sergeant, I could advance no higher as an enlisted man.

Therefore I noticed with interest the announcement of an exam for warrant officer, junior grade—open to master sergeants with 10 years of service. But when I sat down to take the test, I soon realized I would not pass because a large part of it dealt with the B-29 bomber, which I had watched devastate Japan. But my postwar armament experience had been with fighter aircraft at March Field.

Yet I got over my disappointment, and six months later I was able to attend a course on the armament and fire control of the B-29 at Lowry Field, Colorado. Soon after, I took another test for warrant officer, which called for practically the same knowledge of B-29s that my earlier test had required. This time I had no trouble passing. But now I faced the Board of Examiners.

My oral examination seemed to be going well until the President of the Board asked me if I had any recommendations about current B-29 operations. I said, "Yes I do, Colonel." A little surprised, the chairman and the board listened carefully as I explained a shortcoming I'd noticed: "Before B-29s are flown by reserve crews on temporary duty for training, our base armament and fire controllers check all guns and harmonize their operation with the fire control systems so the B-29 is ready for instant combat. Unfortunately, the temporary duty gunners get bored on their training flights and too frequently fiddle around with the gun turrets and negate the effort to keep the planes combat ready."

When he heard this, the colonel looked at one of his officers and exploded, "Is this true, Major?" The major squirmed and said, "I'll have to look into it, sir." The colonel looked at me and ended my exam with, "Thank you, Zincke. That will be all." But he didn't look too happy. As I walked away, I thought I had failed for the second time to become a warrant officer by opening my big mouth. But a couple of weeks later, new regulations appeared on the bulletin board that strictly forbade temporary duty crews from touching the gun controls except during actual training operations. My promotion now seemed possible, but when?

Meantime, the 1st Fighter Group at March Field had been replaced by the 22nd B-29 Bomber Group, so my course on B-29 armament at Lowry Field became very helpful. But I didn't feel so good after the Korean

War started in 1950—I didn't like my assignment to the Far East to inspect B-29 armament and fire control procedures. Looking for a way out, I went up to the office of a friendly sergeant to check the regulations about former POWs being sent back to Japan for service. But the regulations stated that dependants of POWs could not be sent, but the servicemen themselves could. I had no choice so reported to Yokota Air Field near Tokyo in 1951. It was headquarters for the Far East Air Force Bomber Command, which was then actively engaged against North Korean forces.

I arrived at Yokota Air Field hungry but at an odd hour, so when I went into the NCO dining room, no one was eating. After being served, I noticed a long row of Japanese waiters, all dressed in white, standing along the wall. It might have been my imagination, but I thought they were all staring at me. I hastily finished and got out of there—thoroughly spooked because my three years of captivity under the scrutiny and control of Japanese soldiers had seemed to become real again.

Despite this poor beginning, I enjoyed my tour of duty, which involved inspecting armament and fire control records at a number of B-29 bases in Japan and Okinawa. They were engaged in active wartime operations over Korea. Another good part of my tour was my being notified that I had been appointed warrant officer, junior grade.

According to Air Force custom, I handed a dollar bill to the first enlisted man I saw after learning of my promotion. That evening I was planning to take a date to a big dance at the NCO club. But no longer being an enlisted man, I had to be invited, so one of my friends obliged.

Back at March Field I had to take another course because of my promotion. It was the Armaments and Electronics Officers' course—the title of my new position. Each squadron had one of us. But I didn't stay at March Field long.

In 1952 I received orders to report to Alexandria Air Field in Alexandria, Louisiana, which was a tactical air base. Although I was trained to handle B-29s, I didn't point out the mismatch between my experience on B-29s and the fact that Alexandria was a fighter

Warrant Officer Herbert Zincke, June 28, 1952—on armaments inspection tour at Far Eastern Air Force Bomber Command. (Photograph supplied by the author)

air base. In working with B-29s, I had been part of the Strategic Air Command (SAC), which was commanded by General Curtis LeMay. His B-29s had helped bring down Japan, but now his administration of SAC was widely unpopular. At SAC air bases, sloppy salutes or tiny uniform violations meant harsh punishment for enlisted men. Even though I was now a warrant officer, I did not like this tense atmosphere, so I was glad to be going to Alexandria Air Field in Louisiana. Before I left, my first wife and I were divorced.

I had been at Alexandria for three enjoyable years and had married my second wife when puzzling orders came in 1955 to report to Headquarters, Tactical Air Command at Langley Air Force Base in Virginia. When I arrived, I was sent to a Lt. Col. Smith's office for an interview. I had been worried that I had done something wrong to attract the attention of this high echelon of Air Force fighter aircraft, and I was still worried when I entered Smith's office.

He was a large, energetic-looking man and had me sit down. Then he asked, "Do you remember me, Zincke?" To my, "No Sir," he continued, "Well, I remember you from before the war at Hickam Field. You were on my work party that was moving four-man, wooden huts from Luke Field to accommodate the big build-up at Hickam. I remembered you when I was looking over a list of Armament and Electronic officers to find one to serve at the directorate I'm establishing here. I appreciated your help then at Hickam, and you have the right qualifications to help me here."

I was flabbergasted! Here I was being considered for a position about four echelons of control above my slot at squadron level at Alexandria Field. I hadn't remembered the colonel but remembered moving the four-man huts. Now Lt. Col. Smith wanted me to come to Langley, and I felt he would be easy to get along with.

I had settled in my new job at Langley for only a few months when Earl Smith called me into his office and waved a sheet of paper at me. He explained, "This is the report of a fighter gun that exploded on the firing range at your old air base in Alexandria. Go down there and find out what happened." I scanned the report and replied, "I think I know what happened. I'm on my way."

At the firing range at Alexandria air base, I gathered the sergeant and his men who had been firing the gun. I started by saying, "I know exactly what happened. You were checking the bore sight with the instrument that is inserted into the barrel. Then you forgot to take it out before you started to fire." I got only denials at first, but finally the sergeant admitted I was right.

Then, as an afterthought, I looked through the gun sights. But instead of seeing the target set up on the field, I saw cars passing along a highway some distance away. I was shocked, because this meant the guns' range extended at least to the highway—the caliber and range of the guns now being tested exceeded the range facility that had been established for earlier, lesser range guns. I immediately informed the base commander and phoned my boss, Lt. Col. Smith, in Langley. They shut down the firing range until a new one could be established.

Before I retired in 1960, Earl Smith saw that I received a Commendation Medal for my service in the Air Force—I suppose in part for my work on the exploded gun and the too short firing range at Alexandria Air Field. I had served in the Air Corps, and then the Air Force, for 23½ years. I soon started work at Vitro Corporation in Silver Spring, Maryland, where I worked on fire control systems for Navy warships. A few years after starting at Vitro, I heard sad news about my friend and old boss, Earl Smith.

Smith had been promoted to full colonel—unusual for a non–West Point graduate. But he had been forced to retire. He had incurred the anger of his superior, a West Pointer, by housing a group of enlisted men in a hotel to save them from voracious mosquitoes. The men were working outdoors in Florida—setting up the Matador missile system, an important Cold War weapon. Earl Smith was heartbroken and drinking too much when a contractor friend we had worked with at Langley came through with a fine job offer in his company. I was most pleased that Earl had a good position, because we were good friends and I admired him.

I enjoyed my work at Vitro until I retired in 1983. My wife and I lived happily together at our Silver Spring home until she died in 1997. I've had two heart bypasses, one in the past year, but am feeling good and enjoyed a recent reunion of Bataan veterans near the Fontana Dam in North Carolina. My son, Joseph Dollar, drove me there, and I enjoy his company at our home in Silver Spring.

Herbert Zincke (left) and Richard and Peg Beck—remembering some good things about Philippine service in World War II. (Photograph supplied by the author)

Appendix A: Roster of Kawasaki Prison Camp*

Adams, Victor P.
Adamson, Paul V.
Akullian, Arthur   60th Coast Art'y
Allen, Leonard F.   QM, 89th Philippine
Altman, Robert   14th Bomb, 19th Grp
Amo, Robert J.
Angeli, Arthur J.†   30th Bomb, 19th Grp
Armstrong, Don, PFC   4th Marine
Arner, George E.†
Arnold, George   28th Bomb, 19th Grp
Arnold, Max J.   28th Bomb, 19th Grp
Arwood, George   28th Bomb, 19th Grp
Baker, Harold H.   28th Bomb, 19th Grp
Baker, Thurman E.
Bandy, Thos. M., Jr., PFC   28th Bomb, 19th Grp
Barber, Edward   2nd Marine
Bareika, Stanley P.
Barton, Herbert S.
Beymer, Melvin G.†   30th Bomb, 19th Grp
Bibin, Michael   93rd Bomb, 19th Grp
Birmingham, Morris, Sgt.   28th Bomb, 19th Grp
Bishop, Elwin W.
Blackmer, Gerald C., PFC   60th Coast Art'y
Blankenship, Andrey   QM, 89th Philippine

*This roster includes the American, Dutch, and British prisoners at Kawasaki. There were
 also about 140 native Javanese from the Dutch East Indies, now Indonesia.
†Died at Kawasaki

Bogle, K. E., Sub/Lt.   Royal Navy Reserve
Booth, Donald F.   4th Marine
Boyd, Grady   200th Coast Art'y
Bradbury, J. A., T/Sgt.   Army Signal Corps
Bradford, Paul A.
Brandt, L. H., PFC   28th Bomb, 19th Grp
Brindley, Ralph D.†   701st Ord., 19th Grp
Britton, John W., M/Sgt.   28th Bomb, 19th Grp
Brock, Reid H., S/Sgt.   28th Bomb, 19th Grp
Buckem, Marvin C.   28th Bomb, 19th Grp
Budd, Edward W.†   7th Materiel, 19th Grp
Buelow, H. G.†   Died 4/15/43, beriberi.
Burkey, Hilary E.
Burkhardt, Frederick, PFC   440th Ord., 19th Grp
Burnett, William E.   QM, 89th Philippine
Burton, Francis F., PFC   440th Ord., 19th Grp
Busch, Nelson A.   4th Marine
Butterworth, Charles M.   14th Bomb, 19th Grp
Byrum, William F.
Calhoon, William O.
Call, Robert, PFC   28th Bomb, 19th Grp
Callahan, Charles
Callen, Oranda (Ace)
Carnes, Gordon, CPL   28th Bomb, 19th Grp
Carney, Frank J., Ensign or Lt.   Navy, died during 7/25/45
                                     direct hit on Camp No. 2—in
                                     fire party left at barracks.

Casey, Leroy   28th Bomb, 19th Grp
Cashio, Carl   440th Ord.
Catt, Sidney E., Lt.   Royal Air Force
Cavanaugh, Jas. K., PFC   440th Ord., 19th Grp
Chambers, Raymond W., CPL   60th Coast Art'y
Christopher, George, PFC   5th Air Base
Clayton, John D., PFC   28th Bomb, 19th Grp
Clements, Henry B.†   4th Marine, died 3/17/43 of
                                     malnutrition.

Collins, Thomas E., CPL   4th Marine
Cornellison, Henry J.   28th Bomb, 19th Grp
Cox, William A.
Craig, Gaile E.   QM, 89th Philippine
Cross, Charles G.   4th Marine
Cuffle, Kermit S.
Curtin, Dr. A. P., Lt.   Royal Naval Volunteer Reserve
Dakan, Robert E.   28th Bomb, 19th Grp
Daley, Charles E.†   28th Bomb, 19th Grp
Davis, H. D.   4th Marine
Deadrick, Jas. E.

Decker, Wilfrid E.	QM, 89th Philippine
Delucia, Alphonse R.	28th Bomb, 19th Grp
Demoss, Meredith C.	440th Ord.
Didio, Vincent, Pvt.	QM, 2nd Philippine
Diskauski, William R.	QM, 2nd Philippine
Diubaldo, John J.	14th Bomb, 19th Grp
Dodd, Doyle H.	4th Marine
Dorrell, John W.	440th Ord., 19th Grp
Dreher, Alfred B., Capt.	5th Air Base
Duncan, Bertram J.	QM, 89th Philippine
Earles, David L.	5th Air Base
Edmonds, William R.	701st Ord., 19th Grp
English, David K.	701st Ord., 19th Grp
Ervin, William E., Pvt.	
Estrada, Silas E.	440th Ord., 19th Grp
Everett, Kent E.	5th Air Base
Federolf, Kurt, PFC†	14th Bomb, 19th Grp, died during 7/25/45 direct hit on Camp No. 2—in fire party left at barracks.
Felsenthal, Albert	14th Bomb, 19th Grp
Foster, Robert W.	30th Bomb, 19th Grp
Fox, John W., PFC	28th Bomb, 19th Grp
Frank, Elmer L., Pvt.	30th Bomb, 19th Grp
Fronek, Joseph J.	440th Ord., 19th Grp
Fry, Richard L.	701st Ord., 19th Grp
Gallegos, Reynaldo	QM, 89th Philippine
Garcia, Frank C., Sgt.	30th Bomb, 19th Grp
Garity, Thomas E., PFC	4th Marine
Garner, Clell V.	440th Ord., 19th Grp
Gaver, Raymond F.	701st Ord., 19th Grp
Gayle, Ernest F.	QM, 90th Philippine
Gentry, Roy Y., Lt.	14th Bomb, 19th Grp
Giardina, Joseph A.	14th Bomb, 19th Grp
Gilbert, Oliver C., PFC	4th Marine
Gilbert, Richard, PFC	4th Marine
Gilmore, Orville E.	4th Marine
Gomez, Earl B.	QM, 2nd Philippine
Gomme, Verl V.	14th Bomb, 19th Grp
Gonson, Albert S.	28th Bomb, 19th Grp
Gonzalez, Pablo	QM, 2nd Philippine
Goodman, David R.	QM, 89th Philippine
Gordon, H. R., Sgt.	60th Coast Art'y
Grady, Jack	440th Ord., 19th Grp
Gudgeon, Ishmael L.	14th Bomb, 19th Grp
Guy, Richard	
Hahn, Red E.	

Hall, Leo R.	
Halslip, William B.	701st Ord., 19th Grp
Hampton, Thurlan E.	QM, 89th Philippine
Hanson, Julle A.	28th Bomb, 19th Grp
Harp, Stanley K.	93rd Bomb, 19th Grp
Harper, Lloyd, PFC	19th Grp
Hartson, Eugene L.	28th Bomb, 19th Grp
Heimbuch, George, PFC	5th Air Base
Henderson, Jas. C.	701st Ord., 19th Grp
Hensley, Howard G.	4th Marine
Hewson, Wallie J., S/Sgt.	14th Bomb, 19th Grp
Higbie, Benjamin G.	19th Grp
Hixon, A. L., Cpl.	4th Marine
Hoffman, Derwood T.	19th Grp
Holleman, Marshall R.	440th Ord., 19th Grp
Hollenbeck, William J.	
Hough, Richard P.	14th Bomb, 19th Grp
Houston, Ralph L., Pvt.	Medical
Howard, Clyde A.	440th Ord., 19th Grp
Howren, Robert C.	28th Bomb, 19th Grp
Hoy, William F., S/Sgt.	28th Bomb, 19th Grp
Hughes, Jas. R.	30th Bomb, 19th Grp
Hull, Eugene L., PFC	28th Bomb, 19th Grp
Hull, William E., Cpl.	19th Grp
Innis, Leon B.	4th Marine
Irvin, Clair E.	30th Bomb, 19th Grp
Irving, Earest J.	14th Bomb, 19th Grp
Ivey, Joe	30th Bomb, 19th Grp
Jackfert, Eddie, PFC	28th Bomb, 19th Grp
Jacobs, J. C.†	19th Grp
Jaegar, Robert	701st Ord., 19th Grp
Jamier, Robert A.†	28th Bomb, 19th Grp
Johannes, Peter Marcus	Dutch Army
Johnson, Charles L., Sgt.	440th Ord., 19th Grp
Jones, Bobby S.	4th Marine
Jones, John S.	4th Marine
Jones, Max H.	7th Materiel, 19th Grp
Jones, William C.	QM, 2nd Philippine
Kaplan, Sumner L.	28th Bomb, 19th Grp
Kellam, Ray A.	4th Marine
Kendrick, Grant, Pvt.	30th Bomb, 19th Grp
King, Grant O.	QM, 89th Philippine
Kittinger, Gillmer, PFC	28th Bomb, 19th Grp
Knight, William H.†	60th Coastal Art'y
Knox, Albert G.	28th Bomb, 19th Grp
Koenig, Roger I.	30th Bomb, 19th Grp
Kosakevitch, Michael	28th Bomb, 19th Grp

Kovel, Albert G. "Red"	28th Bomb, 19th Grp
Kravitz, Norman, Cpl.	14th Bomb, 19th Grp
Krawieki, Chester V., PFC	14th Bomb, 19th Grp
Kritzon, Walter, PFC	14th Bomb, 19th Grp
Krueger, Oliver W.†	QM, 89th Philippine, died of malnutrition.
Lambert, Arie V.	28th Bomb, 19th Grp
Langdon, George D.	701st Ord., 19th Grp
Lape, Ralph L.	5th Air Base
Lapelle, Milan A., Cpl.†	Died 4/12/44
Leonard, Oscar, PFC	28th Bomb, 19th Grp
Lewis, Herbert C.	440th Ord., 19th Grp
Lewis, William J., Jr.	30th Bomb, 19th Grp
Lockerman, J.	Dutch Army
Long, Vernon R.	5th Air Base
Lontz, Joseph S., PFC	28th Bomb, 19th Grp
Loojen, Abraham, Lt-Cmdr.	CO, Dutch submarine
Lubiewski, Edward F., PFC	14th Bomb, 19th Grp
Lundy, William E., PFC	14th Bomb, 19th Grp
Lyman, Daniel G.	440th Ord., 19th Grp
Mailloux, Donald, F/1	U.S. Navy
Maniere, Ellsworth	7th Materiel, 19th Grp
Manuell, Richard G., PFC	14th Bomb, 19th Grp
Mark, Don	28th Bomb, 19th Grp
Matrin, Walter R.	QM, 89th Philippine
Matthias, Robert C.	QM, 89th Philippine
Maurer, Fred L.	AM, 89th Philippine
McCloud, Morey D.	5th Air Base
McCool, William P., Sgt.	30th Bomb, 19th Grp
McEwen, Keith J.†	30th Bomb, 19th Grp
McGuire, Lawrence, Cpl.	28th Bomb, 19th Grp
McKay, Rod, PFC	
McMullen, Milton L.	701st Ord., 19th Grp
McQain, Clarence E.	5th Air Base
McWilliams, Carl H.	59th Coast Art'y
Meek, Eugene E., PFC	
Mendel, Charles S.	59th Coast Art'y
Mensink, W. H.	Dutch Army
Miller, Marvin L.	QM, 89th Philippine
Mitchell, Harold R.	440th Ord., 19th Grp
Mitchell, Jimmie E.	60th Coast Art'y
Montgomery, Charles E.	7th Mat., 19th Grp
Moore, Donald L., PFC	19th Grp
Moore, Ed McDonald	440th Ord., 19th Grp
Moore, Paul B., Cpl.	440th Ord., 19th Grp
Moore, Vivien E.	59th Coastal Art'y
Morris, Era F.	30th Bomb, 19th Grp

Moss, Wilford A., Cpl.	701st Ord., 19th Grp
Mueller, Jas. J.	30th Bomb, 19th Grp
Munn, Donald A.	U.S. Navy
Murdock, John G., Sgt.	14th Bomb, 19th Grp
Naber, Roelof, 1st Lt.	Dutch Air Force
Nangle, Jas. J.	30th Bomb, 19th Grp
Nauman, Donald L.	28th Bomb, 19th Grp
Neblett, Robert W., Jr.†	14th Bomb, 19th Grp, died 7/6/43 of beriberi.
Nelson, J. M., Sgt.	
Nettles, D. "Pappy," M/Sgt.	5th Air Base
Newsome, Paul E.	701st Ord., 19th Grp
Newton, Charles	QM, 2nd Philippine
Norman, Walter	30th Bomb, 19th Grp
Nuzzo, George J., PFC	Medic
O'Brien, Patrick D., PFC	28th Bomb, 19th Grp
Oliver, John H., PFC	28th Bomb, 19th Grp
Oltz, Andrew J.	28th Bomb, 19th Grp
Oricht, I., M/Sgt.	28th Bomb, 19th Grp
Osborn, Richard J.	19th Grp
Ouelette, Earnest	Medic
Paluch, Stanley J., PFC†	5th Air Base, died during 7/25/45 direct hit on Camp No. 2—in fire party left at barracks.
Parker, Edgar B.	QM, 89th Philippine
Parrish, Ralph	QM, 89th Philippine
Patrick, William L.	440th Ord., 19th Grp
Pecher, Henry B.	12th Recon
Pecynski, Bernard J.	60th Coast Art'y
Pelerek, Felix F.	QM, 2nd Philippine
Peoples, Thomas F.	7th Mat., 19th Grp
Petersen, Richard	14th Bomb, 19th Grp
Phelps, Harold P.	30th Bomb, 19th Grp
Phillips, Robert W.	28th Bomb, 19th Grp
Pierce, Thomas P., Cpl.	28th Bomb, 19th Grp
Ping, Clarence L.	803rd Eng.
Plaskon, Nicholas	59th Coast Art'y
Poulon, Earnest	28th Bomb, 19th Grp
Powell, Oscar M.	28th Bomb, 19th Grp
Pozzani, Mario, PFC	14th Bomb, 19th Grp
Prah, Frank S.	28th Bomb, 19th Grp
Price, Orren G.	5th Air Base
Purcell, Lowell E., Cpl.	30th Bomb, 19th Grp
Quick, Henry D. PFC	14th Bomb, 19th Grp
Raab, Otto E.	5th Air Base
Rabinold, Thomas W.	440th Ord., 19th Grp

Ramirez, A. G., M/Sgt.	5th Air Base
Ramey, Samuel N., Sgt.	30th bomb, 19th Grp
Rankin, L. C.	701st Ord., 19th Grp
Rawlings, Merle T.	701st Ord., 19th Grp
Ray, George C., PFC	14th Bomb. 19th Grp
Raymond, Lester, 1Pvt.	7th Mat., 19th Grp
Reidinger, Raymond, Cpl.	14th Bomb, 19th Grp
Renfro, Robert L.	28th Bomb, 19th Grp
Reynolds, William R.	803rd Eng
Rhaligan, Henry P.	19th Grp
Ricchini, Edwin T.	19th Grp
Richards, C. L., S/Sgt.	440th Ord., 19th Grp
Richardson, J. W., Cpl.	4th Marine
Richardson, Raymond, PFC	5th Air Base
Riddle, P. E., S/Sgt.	28th Bomb, 19th Grp
Riedel, Frank F.	4th Marine
Riley, Jas. M., PFC	440th Ord., 19th Grp
Romollo, Carl J.	440th Ord., 19th Grp
Rubia, Frank	5th Air Base
Russell, Clyde P.	59th Coast Art'y
Sackrider, Oraval L.	60th Coast Art'y
Salazar, Jovancio J.	30th Bomb, 19th Grp
Schmisser, C. W., Cpl.	28th Bomb, 19th Grp
Seres, John, S/Sgt.	28th Bomb, 19th Grp
Shangreuh, L. E.	31st Infantry
Shaver, William H.	440th Ord., 19th Grp
Sheehan, William J., Jr.	28th Bomb, 19th Grp
Shellhart, Marshall S.	701st Ord., 19th Grp
Shelton, Archie H., Cpl.†	4th Marine, died during 7/28/45 direct hit on Camp No. 2—in fire party left at barracks.
Shelton, Herbert R.	4th Marine
Shenaut, A. C., S/Sgt.	701st Ord., 19th Grp
Shepard, John T.	803rd Eng
Sidas, Mike	28th Bomb, 19th Grp
Silverman, Louis, Pvt.	440th Ord., 19th Grp
Simicich, Peter P.	
Smith, Alfred W.	19th Grp
Smith, Earl O.	19th Grp
Solberg, Eugene	701st Ord., 19th Grp
Somerfield, Lawrence E.	QM, 89th Philippine
Somers, Arthur J.	440th Ord., 19th Grp
St. Clair, Marvin	
Stansell, F. M.†	14th Bomb, 19th Grp, died 12/22/42 of dysentery.

Stantz, Frederick D.	440th Ord., 19th Grp
Stapleton, Edward B.	28th Bomb, 19th Grp
Steadman, Edwin S.	4th Marine
Steadman, K. L.	Died in Tokyo of dysentery, possibly soon after war ended.
Stewart, W. R., Jr., Sgt.	14th Bomb, 19th Grp
Stock, Harry D.†	QM, 89th Philippine, died 12/1/42 of dysentery.
Storey, Kenneth, Cpl.	30th Bomb, 19th Grp
Sullivan, Clyde P.	
Supernois, Robert R.	440th Ord., 19th Grp
Swagerty, Thomas F.	701st Ord., 19th Grp
Swartz, Jack W., Lt. (jg)	U.S. Naval Reserve
Tallant, Jas.	440th Ord., 19th Grp
Tannehill, Glen M.	60th Coast Art'y
Taylor, Rogers L.	192nd Tank
Tereletski, Mike, Sgt.	28th Bomb, 19th Grp
Thomas, William H., Cpl.	14th Bomb, 19th Grp
Thompson, John W.†	60th Coast Art'y
Thompson, Wayne, Cpl.	30th Bomb, 19th Grp
Tomczuk, Chester S.	28th Bomb, 19th Grp
Tonchia, John J.	60th Coast Art'y
Trejo, Joe L.	440th Ord., 19th Grp
Trotter, Randall E.†	19th Bomb Grp
Turner, John R., Pvt.	7th Mat., 19th Grp
Van Cleave, Elbert, Cpl.	28th Bomb, 19th Grp
Van Engers, W.	Dutch Army
Venable, Chester, Pvt.	5th Air Base
Vimnessett, Odis E.	59th Coast Art'y
Wagner, Elmer F., PFC	5th Air Base
Wallace, W., Cpl.	Royal Air Force
Wantland, Robert E., PFC	5th Air Base
Warner, Grant T., PFC	14th Bomb, 19th Grp
Watts, Frank S.	28th Bomb, 19th Grp
Westervelt, Ralph, Sgt.	28th Bomb, 19th Grp
Whitley, Billy Joe	28th Bomb, 19th Grp
Wilbur, Charles O., PFC	440th Ord., 19th Grp
Wiley, Harold W., PFC	28th Bomb, 19th Grp
Wilkes, William, PFC†	440th Ord., died during 7/25/45 direct hit on Camp No. 2—in fire party left at barracks.
Wilkins, J. E., PFC	31st Infantry
Wirtz, Frank	
Wolfheimer, Frank, Ensign	U.S. Navy
Woodall, Dwight, Sgt.	28th Bomb, 19th Grp

Wright, Carmio
Wyllsey, Thomas V., T/Sgt.   5th Air Base
Young, Alfred R. (Blackie), S/Sgt. 28th Bomb, 19th Grp
Young, Jerry E.   440th Ord., 19th Grp
Zeib, Marshall C.   14th Bomb, 19th Grp
Zeller, Elmer L.
Zincke, Herbert L., S/Sgt.   14th Bomb, 19th Grp

Appendix B: Kawasaki Defendants at the War Crimes Trials[*]

M/S John Britton stayed in Japan to be a witness at the postwar War Crimes Trials in Yokohama. Because of his and other POW testimony, the tribunal convicted members of the Japanese staff at Camp No. 2 at Kawasaki. The Japanese listed below served while I was there, until July 2, 1945. After that date additional Japanese came, and some were convicted. But by 1956 the total number of incarcerated war criminals who had been convicted of serious offenses was down from 2,000 to 383. Yet even all of these were pardoned and released by December 1958.

Name	Position	Sentence
Lt. Emori[†]	Camp Commander	20 years
Lt. Hayashi	Camp Commander	3 years
(Sgt.) Kasuya[§]	Supplies, clothes	20 years
Kondo, civilian[†]	Interpreter	1 year
Sgt. Mizuno	Top NCO	5 years
Lt. Myazaki	-----	40 years
(Lt.) Saito[§]	Camp Commander	30 years
Sgt. Shiozawa	Top NCO	20 years
Cpl. Watanabe	Medic	40 years

*Ginn, Sugamo Prison, 1992; see Case No. 92, pages 146–147.

†These men were not charged for crimes at Camp No. 2, but for crimes at a British camp before they came to Kawasaki.

§Ginn states that Kasuya and Saito were designated civilians when tried but states such defendants usually served in the military, were wounded, and then reassigned as civilians. See Ginn, Sugamo Prison, page 140.

Bibliography

Birdsall, Steve. *Saga of the Superfortress.* Garden City, NY: Doubleday, 1980.

Braley, William C. *The Hard Way Home (A Coast Artillery Assn. Book).* Washington, DC: Infantry Journal Press, 1947.

Ginn, John L. *Sugamo Prison, Tokyo: An Account of the Trial and Sentencing of Japanese War Criminals in 1948, by a U.S. Participant.* Jefferson, NC: McFarland, 1992.

Holmes, Linda G. *Unjust Enrichment: How Japan's Companies Built Postwar Fortunes Using American POWs.* Mechanicsburg, PA: Stackpole Books, 2001.

Jackfert, Edward, and Andrew Miller, editors. *History of the Defenders of the Philippines, Guam and Wake Island, 1941–45.* Paducah, KY: Turner Publications, 1991.

Kerr, E. Bartlett. *Surrender and Survival.* New York: William Morrow, 1985.

Knox, Donald. *Death March: The Survivors of Bataan.* New York: Harcourt Brace Jovanovich, 1981.

Manchester, William. *American Caesar: Douglas MacArthur, 1880–1964.* Boston: Little, Brown, 1978.

_____. *Goodbye, Darkness: A Memoir of the Pacific War.* New York: Bantam Doubleday Dell, 1979.

Mapes, Victor L., with Scott A. Mills. *The Butchers, the Baker: The World War II Memoir of a U.S. Air Corps Soldier Captured by the Japanese in the Philippines.* Jefferson, NC: McFarland, 2000.

McClendon, Ennis, and Wallace F. Richards. *The Legend of Colin Kelly.* Missoula, Montana: Pictorial Histories, 1994.

Mills, Scott A. *Stranded in the Philippines.* Quezon City, Philippines: New Day Publishers, 1994.

Nordin, Carl S. *We Were Next to Nothing.* Jefferson, NC: McFarland, 1992.

Piccigallo, Philip R. *The Japanese on Trial.* Austin: University of Texas Press, 1979.

Spector, Ronald H. *Eagle Against the Sun.* New York: The Free Press, 1985.

Thomas, William H., unpublished manuscript, Indianapolis, IN.

Time-Life Books. *Japan at War.* Alexandria, VA: Time-Life Books, 1980.

Weiss, Edward W. *Under the Rising Sun.* Erie, PA: The author, 1992.

Index